BLOOMS
and
BUTTERFLIES

Life after Loss

FARIS JEAN ATKINSON

Faris Atkinson
RR #2 Site 5 Box 38
Grande Prairie, AB
Canada
farisjean@yahoo.ca
www.farisjean.com

LIBRARY AND ARCHIVES CANADA CATALOGUING IN PUBLICATION

Faris Jean, 1956-
    Blooms and butterflies : life after loss / by Faris Jean.

Includes bibliographical references.
ISBN 0-9734414-0-2

    1. Bereavement—Psychological aspects. I. Title.
BF575.G7F37 2004   155.9'37   C2004-906906-3

Editing by William Coulthard, Toronto, ON
Cover design by Jordan Walega, Grande Prairie, AB
Design and layout by the Vancouver Desktop Publishing Centre
Printed in Canada by Ray Hignell Services

An Irish Blessing

May the wings of the butterfly kiss the sun,
and find your shoulder to light on to bring you
luck, happiness and riches, today, tomorrow and beyond.

A Verse

A Butterfly lights beside us like a sunbeam,
And for a brief moment,
It's glory and beauty belong to our world,
Then it flies on again,
And though we wish it could have stayed,
We feel so blessed to have seen it.

—Unknown

*This book is dedicated to all
of you who have influenced me
at some time in my life simply
by my knowing you.
You have shaped me.
Thank You.*

Canada's Western Provinces

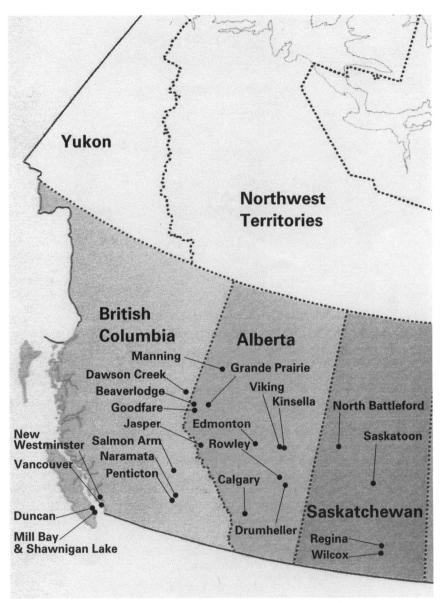

Yukon

Northwest
Territories

British
Columbia

Alberta

Manning
Dawson Creek
Beaverlodge
Goodfare
Jasper
Salmon Arm
Naramata
Penticton

New
Westminster
Vancouver

Duncan
Mill Bay
& Shawnigan Lake

Grande Prairie
Viking
Kinsella

Edmonton
Rowley

Calgary

Drumheller

North Battleford

Saskatoon

Saskatchewan

Regina
Wilcox

Canada's Western Provinces : towns and cities referred to in this book

Contents

Acknowledgments

I want to acknowledge those in my life that had a direct impact on the outcome of this book.

First I need to thank my family. To Terry Atkinson, my husband and partner who has encouraged and supported me to bring this project from an idea to a published book. To Clinton, Erin and Jessie, my beautiful children of whom I am so proud and without them, my life would not be the same. I could not even imagine how very much I have learned from my children. They are true and wonderful blessings for which I will always be grateful.

A special thanks goes to the Suicide Prevention Resource Centre, Grande Prairie, Alberta. They provided me with resources, experiences and emotional support. A large amount of the websites I have included, the tips on how to help a friend, Information on Depression, and more, has come to me through them.

And last, but certainly not least, I have to thank some individuals who, without them, I would not have been able to finish this project.

Thank You to Bill Coulthard, my editor, who stuck by me through thick and thin, past deadlines and over bumps in the road. He continually encouraged and guided me. I am forever grateful for his patience and expertise.

Thanks to Jason Roche, my young dashing knight in shining armour for whom, without his technical skills, I would have lost my book altogether. He retrieved my lost files on two different computers and from CDs and walked me through the dark forest of technology step by step. He has literally been a lifesaver for this project.

To David King, my wise and learned friend, whose gentle encouragement, feedback and love have been great sources of strength to me; I thank you from the bottom of my heart. And to Jordan Walega, another young and talented friend, who created from within his artistic soul a beautiful butterfly for our family. He designed the cover for this book using a version of that very butterfly giving us a cover unique and sentimental, full of symbolism and spirit. Thank you.

Introduction

It is a natural thing we humans do: we tend to gravitate to others with like experiences. We do this for understanding, support, and acceptance, and to share and learn from one another. Even though I could not share a bolt of genius or a brilliant new concept with others drawn to me by our similar tragedies, my ideas seemed new to them. I was asked once, "Who do people turn to? Where do they go after they lose someone?" I realized that those able to help the most seemed to be survivors of grief—and this, maybe, for several reasons.

Imagine you are lost and in pain. Perhaps it is the first time you have suffered a devastating loss. You can't think clearly; your mind is in a haze. The first person or people you think of are those who have suffered a similar experience. My husband and I hear it often: "How do you cope? How did you survive this?" We are the light at the end of the tunnel. We are the hope that life can continue after tragedy strikes. We become a lifeline. We have shared our struggle—and what we learned—with others. We have found that other survivors learned similar coping techniques, but we learned them for ourselves. We have learned of the many support groups and resources available in our communities to help the bereaved, and we have shared that information. It seems, however, that it is easier for people to open their souls and hearts to someone whose understanding comes from walking in the same footsteps. It is we whom they think of first.

Not everyone copes as well as we have. Not everyone is able to share his or her grief and experiences openly, and not everyone has the strength to help others, because everything is too raw. Grief counsellors and other professionals are better equipped to help. People are often not aware of resources available to them, however, and just want a friend. The more time goes by, the more we learn and the stronger we become. It takes a lot of energy to help someone else when you yourself are still trying to heal, but both Terry and I found it in us to do our best to help where we could. I began to realize that maybe what I had to share was valuable to others. This became apparent after a Candle Light Service, December 18, 2002, in Grande Prairie, Alberta, when I was struck by an epiphany: I would write about how I survived losing people who were so much a part of me that I couldn't imagine life without them, and how I am now thriving, gaining strength and flourishing. I have something of value to offer, not just to people who know us or of us and seek us out, but to those who have never heard of us but are lost and saying to themselves, "Where do I go; whom can I talk to who will understand?"

Writing this book was hard for me. I am not special; everyone has a book or more in them. Each person is a collection of stories and experiences. I didn't think I was special enough to write a book until I understood that we all are. It just takes motivation and focus. It took me three years to write this book, which started as a series of essays, stories, and thoughts—venting grief and anger, a type of therapy for me. I had no direction and wasn't sure where it was leading.

It was nearing the end of 2002. Halloween was over; Thanksgiving in Canada was over. The next big holiday would be Christmas. A representative of Oliver's Funeral Chapel and Crematorium approached Terry and me. Would we be interested in being the guest speakers at this December's Candle Light service? They had seen an article in the local paper on my talks to students about depression and suicide. They knew our loss was still quite fresh, but as I was already speaking in public about our experience, perhaps we would consider their invitation. They would really like it if Terry could present a man's point of view. They wanted us both. This funeral home hosts The Candle Light Service every year to provide support, acknowledgement of a difficult time, and to offer hope and peace of mind. It also provides an opportunity for the bereaved to connect with one another at a difficult time of the year. Invitations are mailed to every family who has lost someone within the past year. An open invitation is extended through the media to all who struggle with their grief during the "Festive Season" or who wish to support their friends and family during this time. This non-denominational service consists of music, welcoming comments, acknowledgment of sponsors, a brief prayer, guest speakers, a candle-lighting ceremony and door prizes. It ends in a social with tea, coffee, snacks, and treats. We were honoured to be invited to speak and accepted the challenge.

We had an overwhelming response to our presentation. The newspaper approached us for an interview and, after much discussion, we agreed. We had been amazed at how much what we said helped the people at the service; perhaps we could touch more if we spoke to the paper. We received calls and letters of thanks from that as well. I had never thought seriously about publishing my writing, but as I spoke to more and more people, I remembered that saying, "Write about what you know." I realized that what I know is how to survive loss. What I have to say seems to help. I know how to grieve and cope and I felt a need to share this with as many people as I could. Now I knew the direction of my scribbling. The voices that had been pushing me to write grew louder and all-consuming, "Get at it!" came the voice. "Quit making lame excuses and get it done!" It was then I decided that I would become more structured in my writing and try to get published. There are many books on death and dying, grief and healing, but this book is more than that. It is also some of my history, my story, and my life.

My husband Terry has gone through his journey and helped others as well, but I cannot speak for him. Sometimes I can speak for both of us, or give you my interpretation or "spin" on something we have shared. However, this book is mine; it is *me*. My hope is that, in reading my words, souls reaching out for help as they flail in an ocean of hopelessness and grief will find something to cling to. Please accept these words in the spirit they were written in: with love, compassion and empathy. Here it is, my soul laid bare before you. I am exposed and, in this sharing, I hope you find something you are seeking.

CHAPTER ONE

Agony and Ecstasy

For every action there is
an equal and opposite reaction.
—SIR ISAAC NEWTON

This statement is so very true. There must be balance in the universe—an equal amount of light for every darkness; for every sorrow, an equal joy. Someone asked me if I honestly believed that. And yes, I do. Unfortunately, too many of us are so mired in grief that we are blind to the joys around us. Too often we aren't even looking for that which can make us happy. Sometimes we don't feel we should allow ourselves any joy at all while we are grieving.

Agony and ecstasy seem to be running themes in my narrative. Looking at my life, you may see only one or the other, but most people remark on the agony. They hear my story and believe that I must have been doomed to a life of emotional turmoil and pain—and they say what a strong person I am. I am not any stronger than anyone else, however; I am simply a survivor who has learned that there is balance in the universe. I have also learned to recognize and appreciate the joy that comes my way.

Why do people feel they can't laugh when their hearts are broken? Perhaps it is because it hurts too much to laugh. When you can, maybe you don't let yourself. Why? There are lots of reasons. For some, it may just not seem right to enjoy life when the one they have lost no longer can. For others, it might be social fears: "How will people know how much I hurt if they see me smile?" or "What will people think if I seem to be having a good time so soon after losing someone so precious to me?" Mostly, I think, we don't feel we deserve to be happy.

But there are no rules to grief—no allotted time to cry, no great book stating that it will be time to laugh in six weeks, but only once, and under specific guidelines. I know that sounds ridiculous, but we have laid out a set of rules and we judge one another according to what *we* think is right or how *we* would do something. There is no designated time to feel a certain way or act a particular way. There is no law against finding some happiness amidst the sorrow. People have to understand that everyone and every situation is special. Grief is as unique and different as each of us is.

I have never felt so much pain as I did when I first lost my eighteen-year-old daughter, Jessie; yet now, I have never felt so in touch with the universe, so in tune with my inner spirit, and so happy and content at the prospect of learning more, growing wiser, and travelling further on my amazing spiritual journey. I know I would not be here without first traveling the hard road. I have not reached the ecstasy that balances the agony I still endure, but I feel closer to it every day. As time progresses, a cumulative joy is building and gives me strength.

Many have tried to define life: "Life is like . . ." Well, it could be like many things. Sometimes I see it as walking a balance beam or a tightrope: to move along the beam we must maintain our balance. Some don't realize they need to balance at all, for nothing has ever knocked them off centre. Then something happens that trips them up, something that feels like a blow to the chest or a shove from behind. We stumble and struggle to stay on our beam. If all we see and focus on is what threw us off balance, we tend to fall off the beam—and it is hard to get back on. Sometimes we are hurt so badly by the fall that we can't even try. If we *can* get back on track, it seems we are struggling to maintain our place. Finally we are able to stand without falling, but we may teeter precariously with each step. Moving forward is slow and difficult, but we are at least making progress. The more we recognize the joy that comes our way, the better balance we acquire—until we can stand taller, move more fluidly, and proceed confidently along our narrow path. Each time something comes along to knock us down, our experience helps us stay on our beam. We know how to get back on if we fall off again, and how to keep our balance better. We have grown. Have you noticed how much easier it is to get back on the beam and regain your balance when you have someone to help you—someone to hang on to?

It is the agony that knocks us down and the ecstasy that helps put us back on our feet. Without the ability to find joy in our lives, we flounder and sink deeper into the pit. Then it becomes harder and harder to get back on track.

When I decided to share my life and experiences for use as a balancing pole—something to help folks maintain or find balance—one question haunted me: "Where do I start?"

The answer is to start at the beginning, but the challenge is to determine where the beginning actually is! There are so many beginnings in one's life. Which beginning shall I start from? I don't recall the beginning of this life. I surely don't recall the moment in which my essence was created—my soul, the creation that is me. But I do remember some of the events in my life that changed me, changed my direction or guided me down a different path. These all created new starts for me, but I have discovered that the "beginning" is here right now. There is no time as vital, no moment as precious, as the present. That is where I choose to begin.

I have learned that sorrow, pain and guilt can be debilitating or they can be blessings. I have always felt that I am blessed. Even while others marvel at my "strength," I see myself as just another child of God, another part of creation that on occasion can draw strength from the energy around me to help me move forward. I am no different from anyone else, but I have grown to understand that insight, humility, wisdom, and courage all come out of pain and adversity.

It is easy to let negative emotions mire us. It is easy to get bogged down, wallowing in pain, grief, guilt, fear, and all the emotions and thoughts that lead to bitterness and hopelessness. There we are, mired in a pit of self-pity. We have two choices: stay or leave. Staying is easy, but as long as we stay in our pit, we will continue to add layer after layer of mire. We can justify self-pity and we can relish the sympathy of others. It is easy because we are not alone; many others are with us. They understand and share in our misery. "How are you doing?" we ask our muddy neighbour. "Same shit," is the reply. And we say, "I know how you feel." Then we can go on complaining, even though neither of us is really listening to the other. We are just waiting for them to stop talking so we can pipe back with a story of misery to top the one just told. I heard a wise soul once say that we do not listen to understand, but only to respond. And as this goes on, day after day, the shit gets deeper until it is suffocating.

That's choice number one. Not so nice is it? Why would anyone choose that bitter existence? And yet that is how most of us "live." I have been there. I have been covered in gobs of muck and crap so thick it weighed me down. But I have chosen to pull myself out of it. I want to step out of the mire. It isn't easy; this is where the work really begins, focusing energy on leaving what may be rotten but is at least familiar. There is comfort in familiarity. There is comfort in knowing that there are so many of us here in the mud. Misery really does love company!

So, with every ounce of strength I can muster, I am about to drag myself out of the pit, shake off the muck, and see the life available to me. I want to wash away the shit so thoroughly that when it falls on me again it can't stick. Instead of becoming a heavy layer of muck and manure holding me down, it will become fertilizer at my feet. I will be starting along a new path then: a path of wisdom, compassion, courage, and insight. All those things that make up light and love will grow out of the fertilizer and mud, creating a firm foundation for me to stand on, to walk on, to turn into sturdy stones that build into my life's path with each step I take. That is the life I choose. And that is where you come in. I have taken some important steps to pull myself out of that muddy pit, but I haven't shaken all the shit out of my life. Today, as I start to write, I feel a new beginning. I feel a need to share my journey with you. As each word flies up onto my computer screen, I feel the weight of yesterday transformed into beams of light. To understand me and my philosophies, you need to know what my "shit" is composed of. What is the pain that had me trapped so deep for the last few years that I had only occasional glimpses of light? Where did I get the courage to climb out of the pit? Who has been my inspiration? I am compelled to share this with you—not to try to gain sympathy but to help you understand that, no matter what your story or where your pain stems from, we are all capable of recognizing it as a blessing.

My goal in writing this is to free myself and begin my quest for true self-love and higher spiritual understanding, but I want to inspire others to do the same. We can travel the road together. My footsteps are these little letters on the page as I write; yours will be your own—in your own way and in your own time.

I am a nurturer by nature. It took me some forty years to reach that epiphany. Knowing who one is seems important. It feels good to have a grasp of at least part of who I am. It gives me a starting point. I care deeply for others; I can acknowledge that. I also need to be liked and loved. I found that I struggled with my identity for a long time. Why am I here? What is my purpose? When we are at low points in our lives, those questions rear up and bite us. Remember adolescence? That is when these queries first arose. Then they stay in the recesses of our minds to haunt us again when the going gets tough. So here I am, attempting to nurture again. I guess I thought there would be more to me, but whenever I try to determine what to do next, where to go, what am I here for, it seems to point back to "nurturing". I had to be okay with that.

One day I was especially down. I felt I had no identity. I am a mom, a wife, a registered nurse. I teach first aid and safety courses, have developed safety programs, worked on safety committees, and served as an ambulance emergency medical technician and a volunteer first aid provider with the St. John Ambulance Brigade. So I have some special skills in caring for others or teaching others to care for the sick or injured. But I still felt no sense of identity. When someone asked, "How are you?" I would tell them about my family. How am *I,* anyway? I wasn't sure. As long as I have someone else to worry about and care for, I have purpose and I am okay.

Or am I? Is that enough? I decided that if this is who I am and I recognize that, then I know what brings me pleasure, and that is enough. Love myself for that. Don't make excuses for it. There is no need to justify or defend it. I am a nurturer. That is who I am and it is good. I have learned that many parents, especially mothers, go through this same thing after a loss. We are driven to make sure everyone else is okay first. Then, maybe two years later, when the rest of the family is on the road to good health, it's Mom's turn to crash. This is normal. Watch for it and be ready to help her when she needs it most.

As I walked and wondered who I was and why I existed, a poem formed in my mind:

One day while I was feeling lost
Unsure of what to do
Not knowing my true purpose
My thoughts soon turned to you.

I prayed, "My God, please strengthen me,
And tell me who I am"
Then I knew within my heart
There's no need to understand.

All that is needed is purest love
Unconditional and true
God is love and God's in us
Love's all that we need do.

And then I knew my purpose.
At once it all was clear.
To offer that part of God in me
And to accept it without fear.

I know that my greatest gifts
Are the ones that are gifts to me
And of all my many precious gifts
There are a special three.

And these I offer to the world
One by one at their own time
They are children of God and earth
And they are each a child of mine.

My son I offer to the world
His generosity and his caring
Overflowing with quiet understanding
Heroic in his loving and his daring.

My princess who I really thought
Was mine alone to keep
She taught me and is teaching me
The truth in what I seek.

My Sweet Pea with her courage
Already she's done great things
So young and yet a messenger
Amazing joy she brings.

All these are my offerings
My purpose clear and true
God shared these jewels from Her crown
And their treasure sparkles through.

The best I have to offer
The best I have to give
The best I hold within me
Is that which helps me live.

The life within my spirit
The lives I have to share
The greatest gifts I offer
Are these that I hold dear.

But here's the catch; I had to learn the hard way that there is a difference between helping someone and carrying their load for them. My heart says, "I don't want you to feel bad; let me feel bad for you so you won't hurt any more." But that is the mistake. I can't take away anyone's pain. All I can do is lighten it by letting them know how much I care and sending them love to give them strength. If I try to share their pain, I just add to my own load. Now I'm carrying their pain on top of my own. There are a lot of us, the "nurturers", who get caught in this trap. I didn't recognize it until the load was almost too much for me to bear.

CHAPTER TWO

One of My Beginnings

I have learned that what I *believe* to be real is my own reality. Take memories, for instance. An event occurs that I am involved in or witness. You are there as well. My recollection of that event is based entirely on my interpretation, my perspective, my belief about what occurred. And this belief is entirely personal, unique to me. The same applies to you. When we recall the event later, my memory of it is real and accurate for me, but your memory of the same event may be completely different—and very real to you. Neither memory is wrong. In fact, if we take the time to listen, we can share the different interpretations and thus learn, grow and become enlightened by another person's insights. Instead, we tend to argue about whose memory is "correct." We walk away upset at each other. Such an opportunity lost!

With this in mind, I want to share with you *my* reality, remembering that this is unique to *me*, and anyone else sharing that moment may have a different idea of how it all came to pass.

This is one of my beginnings. It happened in June of 1974, and I became a new person as a result. It didn't happen overnight, but in a blink of an eye.

I can see him still. His back is to us. I'm sitting with my boyfriend, snuggled together and holding hands. My mom is sitting across from us. I can feel her smile. Now that I think of it, I'm sure she was fighting back a few tears. She wasn't saying much that I recall. We had all talked in the car traveling from our home in Beaverlodge, Alberta, to the Dawson Creek airport in British Columbia. I don't recall much of the conversation. After all, these were my parents. I took them for granted and tuned them out at times. I was eighteen and in love with the boy next to me, whom I wasn't going to see for a few months. My attention was on him. I remember cuddling in the back seat on the way to the airport, my parents up front. Dad was driving. I remember being quiet. I was excited about going to work at Naramata in the Okanagan Valley in BC for the summer, but I was nervous, too. It was my first real job and the first time I'd be away from home for very long. But I was focused on the separation from Terry. I held on to him as if I was never going to see him again. I said little for fear that I would start to cry. I was already tearing up from time to time. Terry gave me a little jewel box and, if I recall correctly, it contained a simple and elegant sliver necklace with a little pearl pendant. I don't know what became of it. At the time it was the most precious thing. But the eyes of my memory keep drifting back to the airport, where I see my dad looking out the window toward the tarmac, watching the plane land that was going to carry me away from them. He was leaning against the window frame, staring out through the glass. I didn't pay much attention at the time, but now I see it so clearly. As the plane landed, Terry, Mom, and I wandered over to join him. He reached out with his big warm arms and pulled me to him. I felt his warmth and strength and breathed in his scent of Brylcreem and Old Spice. We both looked at the plane as we hugged. The clearest memory of that day was when Dad turned to me and said, "Well, that pilot landed that plane nice and smooth. I guess he's good enough to carry my little girl." Goodbyes were exchanged, hugs and kisses, and I could feel those three watching me as I boarded and found my seat. I tried to see them out the tiny window and I thought I could make out their figures standing inside against the large glass pane, but it may have been just a comforting image I built myself. My mind keeps going back to seeing my dad, watching out the window as the plane was landing. I hear his words; I see Mom smiling. Did I say, "I love you?" I don't remember. All I know is that those were the last moments and words that we would share. I had held on to Terry as if we would never see each other again.

I wish I had taken the time to savour each moment with my parents instead, because Terry and I have been together for all these years but I never saw my parents again.

I had been at Naramata Centre for Continuing Education for only a matter of days. Naramata, which was sponsored by (but certainly not limited to) the United Church of Canada, was a summer tradition for our family. We always spent at least one or two weeks each summer at this little spot across the Okanagan Lake from Summerland, B.C. But this year I would be staff, and already I was enjoying it. I was being oriented as a youth-group leader. We had already been put to work organizing activities for kids and spending the mornings with them. Over the summer, a new group of families would be coming in each week, and we would be in charge of leading the kids in entertaining and educational activities to help us all in our journey toward spiritual growth. I had already found a niche as a sing-song leader, standing in front of the guests with my guitar (which I named Ben) and the other youth-group leaders, lifeguards, and grounds staff, all belting out spiritually uplifting songs—a bit of gospel, a touch of pop, and a lot of folk.

What a sight! It was 1974. One young fellow looked up at me with big brown eyes and said: "I want to be a hippie just like you when I grow up!" I never really thought of myself as a hippie—that era had pretty well run its course—but when I look at old pictures I can see

Terry Atkinson and Faris Swallow, 1975.

where he got that idea. My hair is thick, with a natural curl. I could never grow it long and straight like my friends, but at that time it was to my shoulders. This is as long as it would ever get, and then it would grow outward, like a bushy, unruly mane. My jeans were full of rips, especially at the hem because the fad was to buy overlong pants, wearing them ragged as they dragged in the dirt and gravel. Patches covered some of the tears and these were colourful, usually depicting peace signs, yin and yang, flowers and such. My cut-offs were just that—when jeans became too tattered or the leg style was outdated, the pant legs were cut off and the jeans were worn as shorts for a while longer. I usually had on a tie-dyed shirt, peasant blouse, or halter top to finish the ensemble.

My usual accessory was my guitar slung over my shoulder so that it rode on my back as I walked from place to place. Maybe I *was* a hippie!

I shared a room in MacLaren Hall with Lynette Schultz. She was older than I and, at the suggestion of her minister (my dad), had gone to the winter session at Naramata. She thought the world of Dad and told me once how she felt he had literally saved her life by the help and guidance he had given her. One of the best pieces of advice she felt he had given her was to attend winter session. It sounded like such a wonderful adventure and she would tell me stories with sentiment and enthusiasm as we talked at the end of each day. She had loved Naramata so much that she stayed on as summer staff. I'm not sure what her job actually was, but I know she drove the van over the winding nine-mile road overlooking the Okanogan Lake to Penticton and back. She ran errands, chauffeured people, and delivered supplies all over. I would dream about going to winter session, too, when I was finished school. I was a year behind her and had my Grade 12 to finish, but I couldn't wait to live some of the experiences Lynette was telling me about. On the other hand, I was looking forward to spending more time with Terry and wasn't sure I could stand being away from him for the same length of time as an extended school semester! But I had the summer to enjoy first; there was lots of time to make decisions. Besides, life always throws you curve balls and changes your course when you least expect it, and I was a "go with the flow" kind of gal. I guess I still am in most ways.

It was June 27. I had just got off the phone with Terry. I was in my room boring Lynette with the love-struck ranting of a teenager. She seemed interested and never let on that what I had to say was unimportant. Then we heard skipping steps coming down the hallway. Our room was at the end of the hall and close to an exit leading onto a field that at this moment was the venue of a rousing (and sometimes confusing) game of Naramata baseball. We were used to hearing footsteps of people heading out that door, but these steps were almost dancing. We had to see what was up. It was Elaine Peacock, one of the adult leaders and full-time staff members. Naramata is a First Nations name meaning Smile of Manitou (God), and at that moment I surely felt God smiling on me, I was so filled with joy. Elaine had gathered up someone as she moved through the building, and there were the two of them, arms over each other's shoulders, skipping and dancing toward us. We stepped out of our doorway and asked what was going on. She said Ivan wanted to talk to me, and she gathered us up, spun around, and we started the same skipping dance back the way she had come.

Ivan Cumming and his wife, Nina, were the directors of Naramata. Summer staff didn't usually have much to do with them except in passing. They were always fun and friendly and approachable, but busy with the important job of administration. As summer staff, we had our own people we worked with on a regular basis.

But Ivan and Nina were also close friends of Mom and Dad, so I didn't wonder too much about why the "boss" would send for me. I started to think maybe I had done something wrong and, as I was his friends' daughter, he was going to address the matter in person. That thought especially ran through my head when we encountered Ivan. We grabbed him up in our skipping group and he took a few steps with us, but then quit skipping and silently put his arm around me to guide me away from this happy group. We had turned around again and so were now walking toward the exit by my room. I remember trying to make conversation, but he didn't speak. It was then I feared for my job. What could I have done? It must be bad. He seemed so upset; he was not his usual jolly self. He hadn't skipped with us, and now he wasn't joking, or even smiling. We had walked out of the building and were standing on the huge expanse of grassy lawn separating MacLaren Hall from the road that ran parallel to the beach ahead of us. The director's home was to the left through the trees and it seemed as if we might be walking that way. He stopped and turned to me. I can still see his face as he spoke, but the exact words are not with me. What we said to each other there went something like this:

Ivan said, "Your parents were in a car accident today."

"Are they . . . ?"

"They were both killed."

Stunned at first and knowing Ivan's sense of humour, I thought this wasn't a very good joke at all! Then, realizing by his face and moist eyes that this was real, I wept.

"No, No," I blurted, crying and holding on to Ivan with all my might. We both held on tight as though our embrace was the only thing holding us to the earth—I don't know how long

"Was anyone else with them?"

"No," said Ivan, "they were alone in the car."

"What happened?" I asked. "Was anyone in the other car hurt?" I can't recall how I knew or whether I just guessed that another car was involved.

"No one else was killed," Ivan said. "I think the person in the other vehicle might have some minor injuries."

"Thank goodness they're okay," I said.

I remember crying for some time, asking questions, holding Ivan, and crying some more. Ivan said we should go to the house, as Nina was there and they were trying to get whoever was at my home in Beaverlodge on the phone. There were other people in the house, too. I think Lynette was told and showed up after a while, but the memories of this are like looking through a clouded mirror that keeps moving and shaking. I can't focus on any faces or voices, just the phone. I remember the smell of the plastic, the smooth feel of it in my hand as I spoke to my sister, Heather, on the other end. Considering she was only sixteen and had just learned she had lost her parents, she sounded pretty calm and in control.

It seems to me she held it together because she was the oldest one at home at the time and the younger ones needed her to be strong. "LeeAnn," Heather told me in matter-of-fact tones, "is running around outside on the lawn screaming. There are people trying to calm her down, but she's out of control." I asked about Marilyn and Curtis, but I guess they were visiting friends and weren't home yet.

LeeAnn had turned fifteen just two weeks earlier. Marilyn was twelve, and Curtis, our baby brother, was ten. The five of us had been orphaned in a blink of an eye, a blind spot in the road, rainy weather and a pickup passing a grain truck only minutes outside Beaverlodge. Dad had had his first accident ever, a head-on collision. I'm told they were killed instantly, but I think people say that to make us feel better. I have heard rumours that Mom was alive for a while, but I don't know that for sure. I don't think it really matters. It would be nice to know the truth, but in the end, they left this world and we five were on our own.

Or were we?

Lynette walked me back to our room and helped me pack. It seemed like no time before Lynette and I were in an airplane heading back to Grande Prairie. Lynette's parents, Frank and Ginny, were there to meet us, and so were Dawn and Dr. Don Faris, a geneticist at the Canadian Agricultural Research Station in Beaverlodge.

The Farises have always been very special people in our lives, just as Naramata had been a very special place. Dad met Don at Naramata in the early 1950s. He also met Mom there. Don stood up with Dad when he married Mom on November 6, 1954. Dad had stood up for Don, too. When I was born in April 1956, I was named after two people my dad admired: Don Faris Jr. and Don Faris Sr. It was good to see Dr. Don and Mrs. Dawn there and to be looked after. I didn't have to think about where I was going, how to get there, what I was going to

The Swallow family, March 1974.
Curtis 10, Irene 41, Marilyn 12, Heather 16, Lee Ann 14, Clinton 47, Faris 17.

eat, or anything! It would be years before I could appreciate all the things people had done. There were so many people from Dad's Alberta congregations in Beaverlodge, Hythe and Wembley that I'm not sure what they did to help; I just know they did. People from pastoral charges—in Edmonton and Viking/Kinsella, Alberta; in Mill Bay/ Shawnigan Lake on Vancouver Island; and in Salmon Arm in British Columbia's Shuswap Valley—all helped us in some way, large or small. I don't recall faces or names of all these people, but that doesn't diminish my gratitude for all they did for us when we needed them most. Some decisions were made for us that I wish had been different. We made some ourselves that maybe we should have taken more time to think through. Some decisions we made under pressure. In the end, everything was done out of love and concern for us, even though it may have seemed that some folks "helping" us had their own agendas.

The point is that we had a place to stay, food to eat, clothes to wear. We were given opportunities to make some important decisions on our own, not the least of which was the choice of coffins, burial or cremation, scatter or bury, where they should be interred, and such. (Thank goodness we knew much about our parents' wishes; most were spelled out in a will). We had time together at Naramata to choose where we were going to live—there were many offers—and I still had my summer job there. We had all this because we really weren't alone; we were just without parents. We were grieving and going through transitions—hormones, growing up, lovesickness, changing from child to teen and from teen to adult, all mixed into a stew of pain and intense loss. We were going to be much more work than some people who wanted to finish raising us could handle, despite their best intentions. Bless them all! It turned out that we made some pretty good choices. I spent the summer in the dorm, while my siblings lived with Ivan and Nina. Afterwards, I went back to Beaverlodge to be with Terry and finish high school, and the rest went to live on Vancouver Island with the Garnett family, members of the congregation in Mill Bay and friends of the family.

Do you believe in serendipity, destiny, coincidence, or the wondrous mysteries of the universe? Sometimes things seem to happen for a reason, as if there is an order in the world that guides us through life.

My life seems to show a pattern of this kind of thing. Is it just my imagination? Whatever it is, it is my reality, and you can take it as you wish.

Mom and Dad were about to make a big change in their lives. They were preparing for it, a new life. Dad had quit the ministry. He was going into what he called a "new ministry". They were moving to Rowley, Dad's hometown, about half an hour's drive from Drumheller, Alberta. There they would revamp the old but sound livery barn into a home and bring troubled city kids out there to live with us. The kids would receive counselling from Dad and TLC from Mom. They would have chores and learn how to value themselves. Eventually, there would be family counselling and a "dude ranch" that financially challenged families could enjoy.

That was the dream. It looked as though it would become a reality. Swallow Downs it would be called. Suiting, as Swallow was our surname. Grants had been given and donations collected. Dad had one more Sunday to preach in the three-point pastoral charge of Beaverlodge, Hythe and Wembley, and the congregations had hired a new minister to start after we had left. Dad had been the Protestant pastor at the Air Force Base on the hill, and they were throwing Mom and him a farewell party on June 27, 1974. It was raining, and maybe that was the reason Dad took the highway. He always went up to the base using the back roads, but not this day. He had never had an accident and prided himself on his driving, but it only takes one mishap—and the best driver in the world may not be able to avoid it.

I had turned eighteen in April and was now an adult by law. Mom and Dad had told us about their will, what would happen to us if something happened to them, how they wanted their bodies handled and why. Mom had mentioned that they were going to change their will now that I was legally an adult, but they didn't say how and they never had time. I was to return to Beaverlodge after my summer at Naramata and live in a basement suite with my girlfriend, Linda. The reason was simple. I was old enough to be on my own, I wanted to graduate from high school with my friends, and I wanted to be close to Terry. So the family was "ready" for me to fly the nest. School was just finished and holidays in full swing, but there was still a full summer ahead. Terry was invited to go to the party with my folks, but the D8 Caterpillar tractor that he and his brother had been working with broke down at the last minute. They had to go to Grande Prairie for parts and had to wait for quite a while before getting them. Because of all this, Terry had to cancel his date with my parents. The stage was set; everything was ready.

Let's see, did we forget anything? The oldest is of legal age, the church has hired a new minister, no one is expecting them at another pastoral charge, they are very much in love so they'll have to go together, he'll take the highway instead of the back roads, they'll be alone, and visibility will be poor. The kids are out of school for the summer but will have time to find a new home before school starts in the fall. Money designated for Swallow Downs could easily be swung into a fund for the kids. The oldest has a place lined up and has found her one true love. Yep, that sounds well organized. Let's do it.

Am I stretching it a bit? It's true, but kind of spooky, don't you think? And that's only one event in my life laced with "coincidence" or "mysteries of the universe." Dad didn't believe futures are plotted out in some big book of events somewhere; neither do I. But you have to admit that, even though we have the extraordinary gift of free will and can make our own choices, time and space are linked to all of us in ways we cannot comprehend, and we are linked together as unique creations. As I've said before, everything happens for a reason, and there is balance in the universe. Sometimes connections are more apparent than at other times. This may be because we have enough puzzle pieces to be able to see what the overall picture is supposed to look like, or because our vision is clearer at some times than at others. Whatever the cause, I see many connections binding my life together like silken threads forming a beautiful patchwork quilt. The events woven through my parents' passing were my first glimpse of this "quilt of my life." I'm sure it had been in production for some time; I had just not seen it before. Now I am looking at each little patch to see what it is made of and how it will fit together into the quilt. I believe that, when I reach a certain point in my journey as one of God's creations, I shall actually be able to see a picture or a message sewn right into my quilt. The quilt will actually be a part of something larger: perhaps my quilt connects to yours and many others along the way.

All our quilts get sewn together with threads of love and light, until all the holes in the universe are pulled together and we are once again drawn into complete oneness with the source of all creation: Pure Unconditional Love, God.

Thinking back, my siblings and I were being prepared for Mom and Dad to leave early. One of the most amazing things for me was to receive letters from Mom and Dad to help us through our grief. They were actually written for Grant (Gunner) & Lois Garnett when they lost their oldest and youngest sons in a boating incident off the west coast of Vancouver Island. They had five sons: Blair, David, Steven, Murray, and Tim. The family went with friends—a man, his young son, his father and a friend—to see the sea lions. The seas were rough and the boat overturned.

They were lucky that anyone survived. Blair and David saved them from drowning right away by pulling people up from under the boat and having them hang on to the hull of the overturned vessel. Blair, a strong swimmer, set out for shore for help because no one knew they were in trouble. But Blair didn't make it, and those at the boat were rescued by passing fishermen. Timmy died of hypothermia, and two members of the other family died. Blair's body was found days later. The rest of the family had several days' recovery in hospital. We were living in Edmonton at the time, and this was the first real loss I remember that touched our family, especially me. I had had a childhood crush on Blair when we lived on the Island, and it didn't seem real that someone so strong, young and smart could be gone. Mom and Dad each wrote Lois and Gunner to express their sympathy. Lois gave these letters of comfort to me after Mom and Dad died. What a wonderful gift. I will share them with you now.

My dad wrote:

> 8208 - 123rd ave.,
> Edmonton 20, Alberta
> July 23, 1969

> Dear Lois and Grant,
> Twenty times, or more, I've allowed other items to crowd in ahead of this letter, and still it's difficult to find words. How I wish that there was no need to write, yet all our hoping cannot turn the clock back, and what is done is done.

Words of comfort and encouragement seem shallow in my mind, and look futile on paper. The only real desire, the only true comfort is the impossible return of your two boys and your two friends. It's like a nightmare, and one keeps hoping to wake up and find that all is just as it was; with strong, efficient, sincere Blair quietly going about his chores and making his plans for the future; and Tim excitedly filling his day with a variety of happy activities; with Grant still dreaming impossible dreams—and then making them come true, and Lois, quietly "spoiling" her last son with an overflow of love and generosity.

Thank God you were so full of love and generosity; at least one small bit of comfort is in the knowledge that you had made life on earth a little bit of heaven for Tim—and I suspect the same thing was true for Blair. Perhaps, also, there is some small comfort in the realization that they created a bit of heaven on earth for both of you.

If ever there was any doubt about some dimension, or time, or space known as heaven, then it must now flee. For how could there be a God so cruel as to allow us to create bonds of love this deep and strong without provision for them to extend beyond our brief human existence. And if there was any question as to qualification for the Kingdom of Heaven let it now be answered once and for all. God's capacity for love and forgiveness and sympathy and concern exceeds anything we can know; so it is greater toward Blair and Tim than your own. You had them to love and care for—and to be loved and cared for in return—for a short time, now be certain of this; God has received them to himself.

Though tears roll from my eyes when I think of the loss, still my greatest concern now is for you and the family. Irene and I wish we could be with you, because we share your loss deeply—as do our girls. They keep talking about it, hardly believing that it is true. Had we known that you were going to be home in time for the funeral, I would have flown down. Not because I could do anything more—or better—than Dr. Parsons, but just so as to be there with you in that trying hour.

Now the long nights and days begin. "Why?" and "If!" will spring into your mind night and day unless there can be satisfactory answer or comment made. But who am I to try to comment on these? Just a friend who hopes and prays that he won't ever have to face such tragedy in his own family. But if I do, I hope to have friends who, standing close to me in thought yet sufficiently removed to be able to reason without the soul-wrenching emotion of personal loss, will answer the burning questions for me. So, for you, I tackle the "Why?"

It didn't have to happen. God had not willed it. It was not written nor set in the stars, nor in some great heavenly book, nor a great computer in the sky. (But you know all this.) It didn't have to happen, but it did. If we could look ahead, if we could anticipate, then perhaps we could avoid—but we cannot. The future with its sorrows and its joys remains unknown. It happened because there was a wave at the wrong time or in the wrong place, and because there were rocks, and undertow, and distance, and perhaps several other things, which all together created disaster. There's no comfort in this now, but at least it may help to remove self-blame, which brings us to "If".

If you had not gone out at all! —But life is full of dangers; we cannot refrain from everything that has a potential disaster quotient. So, you drive, you go fishing, boating, swimming, riding, flying or walking, and you take your chances, using all your knowledge, heritage, reflexes, and all other given or earned qualities to see you safely through.

If that is not enough, then what is required is strength and guidance from the source of all power and wisdom, God Himself. Not that God should be left to last, nor that He was, but that when all else fails, where else can you turn?

So we look to God for direction, understanding, and strength. You will face today and tomorrow, building on yesterday's disaster, knowing and feeling that there can still be purpose and value in living. Knowing that sacrifice was made in love, and that somehow, by the grace of God, that sacrifice will not be futile.

Well! You might have known that a preacher must preach, even when he's a friend, and I've preached my sermon of comfort and hope, and I pray that it does give you just that.

Sincerely

Clint.

Imagine it: Grieving the sudden loss of your father and mother in a tragic car crash and reading these words of comfort from the very person you have lost! I ask you, what an amazing blessing is that? Do you know of anyone so blessed? I am—I am that blessed. It never ceases to amaze me and I am forever grateful for parents who were such good friends and to those wonderful friends who chose to share these letters with us.

Now hear what my mother had to say. A selected verse is on the front of the card that she chose. It says:

What God Hath Promised

God hath not promised skies always blue...
Flower-strewn pathways all our lives through.
God hath not promised sun without rain,
Joy without sorrow, peace without pain...
God hath not promised we shall not know
Toil and temptation, trouble and woe.
He hath not told us we shall not bear
Many a burden, many a care.
But God hath promised strength for the day,
Rest for the labourer, light for the way...
Grace for the trials, help from above,
Unfailing sympathy, undying love."

—Unknown

My Mother wrote:

Dear Lois & Grant;

This must be the hardest letter I've ever tried to write. My thoughts have been with you constantly since that first phone call.

Clint was ready to catch the next flight but we were told you were all in hospital and not expected home before the funeral.

I've tried to compose some comforting thoughts and all I find is the empathy of motherhood and the wonder of how could I go on without Faris & Curtis. As I said to Adelaide[1], even though we love each child for himself, there seems to be something extra special about the oldest and the youngest. One seems to strive for perfection in their eldest and the youngest we try to keep a baby —just a little longer!

I took pictures the day Tim came to keep Curt company in that crowd

---

1 Adelaide was a family friend and congregant.

of girls[2] & they are more precious than ever now. And how pleased Tim was for the ride in "Lotus"[3] with Padre Pike[4]. Memories are truly a God-given treasure! You'll have so many within your loving family fellowship—I'm sure your treasure is great.

Blair was such a wonderful boy. I could not help but covet a son like him.

Like so many great heroes of other days, he gave himself for others. We will always feel we were truly blessed in knowing him. Clint always felt that when Blair took on a job, he could forget about it, knowing it would be well done.

One of the shortest statements in Corinthians is "love never ends" So I know our love for the boys will go on to infinity.

This has been a terrible ordeal for you but you must know how many friends and relatives are sharing this with you. Your burden of sorrow has to be lighter with so many to help you.

You are also most fortunate in having three fine sons who will also be helping you to live again. We mothers have much to be thankful for in the dreary, day-to-day chores required by our family. So many things just must be done! Time does dim the ache but my grandmother, who lost a child fifty-odd years ago, still recalls the memory so vividly, she weeps when she thinks too long on the details.

My prayer for you is that David, Murray and Steven will give you such love & joy that your hearts will be full & overflowing with the lives you are living, that this tragic happening may dim & that you are full only of happy memories of these dear ones who have gone to the 'place prepared for them'.

Our Comfort is in knowing God loves them more than we could ever love and they are happier than we could ever make them.

This doesn't make me weep less and somehow I feel it should, but my sympathy seems to be a steady flow of tears.

Our love to you all, Irene.

---

2 The girls were guests at a birthday party for one of my sisters at our home in Mill Bay, Vancouver Island. Tim was invited so that my brother, Curtis, would have someone to play with.

3 "Lotus" was Padre Pike's Lotus sports car.

4 Padre Pike was a retired Baptist minister, born in 1900 and a life-long bachelor. He probably picked up his nickname, Padre, during wartime service, possibly with the Royal Canadian Navy. I haven't found anyone who can confirm this as the people I know met him long after he left the military. We children knew him in his sixties as Uncle Harry, and we were probably the only people who didn't call him "Padre."

These original, hand-written letters are two of the most precious items I have. I keep them in my china cabinet in an envelope. One day I will put them in a safe deposit box. I have a fear of losing these to fire or fading. I feel much better having transposed their contents into this book, as at least the words won't be lost, and now even more people can benefit from them.

Remember I said that we aren't really alone? I know that my siblings had people who helped them in special ways to deal with life, and I know they all had issues, pleasant and happy experiences and hurtful ones, but they were on Vancouver Island. I was in Beaverlodge. They spent the first year with Grant and Lois Garnett and their boys, and then went to live with Tom and Tracy Barry, not too far from there. I think Marilyn lived for a while with the Sullivan family, the parents of one of her school friends. As time went by and they grew up, they left their new homes and made their own way in the world. All this time I was in Alberta, in Beaverlodge, Goodfare, and Grande Prairie. One of my sisters said it felt as though they lost me, too, because I wasn't with them. But my plan had been to stay in Beaverlodge, and so I had. I guess I had been pretty selfish and really didn't realize the effect of my being separated from them. I had my own issues, though. I needed to grow up, finish school and grieve. I have huge holes in my memory; I am recognizing how powerful an eraser grief can be. Those agonizing years are made up of bits and pieces of memories for me. I hear people recall things we did and I can't remember at all. Sometimes I don't even remember the person telling me the memories! It is scary sometimes, but I guess it is natural. It was traumatic, and I couldn't have got through all this without three supports: My faith, Terry, and Terry's Family, the Atkinsons.

My faith was one of the gifts my parents gave me. It was a part of life, of who we were. Dad was a minister in the United Church of Canada, so faith was his life and he transferred it to us in how he lived. He was an amazing man. When I was sixteen, I was a handful. I went through a period of rebellion and was blessed again to come out of it pretty much unscathed. There were times I doubted God's existence and wondered about different interpretations of religions and scriptures. I would talk to Dad. What I admired most about him was how he would answer my questions with a question and get me to think. I would ask, "What do you think?" and he would tell me that what he believed wasn't the issue. I needed to discover my own beliefs, not take on someone else's.

When pressed, he would tell me what he thought, but explain why he thought that way and how it worked for him. I should have my own good reasons why I believe as I do, and "because Dad did" wasn't good enough. I remember one time telling Dad that I didn't think God existed. One of my main reasons was that I couldn't see Him.

Dad asked me if I believed in electricity. I laughed and said, "Of course!"

"Why?" he wanted to know.

"Because I can see it."

"Are you sure? Can you really see electricity? You can see the light it causes, the wires it travels. You can see all the things it does, but can you actually see it? No. You just see the many things it does, so you know it is real."

I have never forgotten that, and it has been the foundation of my faith. I always appreciated the things my father taught me and have tried to teach my children the same lessons.

When Clint first went to Notre Dame in Wilcox, Saskatchewan, to go to high school at age sixteen, he was concerned about attending a Catholic School, having to take Christian Ethics classes, and going to compulsory Mass. I remember telling him—and Jessie and Erin, too—that learning something and believing in something are two very different things.

"Knowing increases your understanding, and therefore your tolerance," I said. "Most of the world's problems today are based on intolerance spawned out of ignorance. Learn as much as you can. You will benefit from it."

And they did. Clint and Erin still are learning and benefiting.

A lot of my wisdom comes from lessons I learned from my father. I was indeed blessed to have parents like mine. I learned to have an open mind, to ask questions and search for answers. They gave me many valuable tools to help me cope with what life threw my way.

Thank God life threw me Terry. My mom loved him. I think she saw in him a man very much like my father. Terry is not a religious person, and he certainly wasn't then, and although I never knew it then—and Terry probably didn't either—I think Mom picked up on the fact that Terry is a highly spiritual man. He is exceedingly generous and thoughtful of others, a farm boy who knows what it means to work hard and have little of material value. A driven, intelligent man who is a high achiever and perfectionist, he drives me nuts, and I love him with all my heart. That is very much like my dad, too. Terry and I were barely eighteen when Mom and Dad died. We were raised very differently, but both of us got the most important thing: we each had a loving, close family. I never worked a lick in my life and was very naïve about the ways of the world. I was protected and raised in a Disney movie! Mom and Dad never fought, and I thought that was normal. Families on TV didn't fight either. I didn't realize that spouses fought at all; I had never seen it.

Terry Atkinson beside his Laterno at Procter and Gamble Pulp and Paper Mill, Grande Prairie Alberta, 1975.

Terry worked hard from the moment he could because everyone in his family had to; there was no choice. There was ample love in his home, but his folks fought too—a much more realistic experience than mine. He had already been a farmer, hunter, and ranch hand, and had worked in logging camps and mills by the time he was sixteen. Terry was five credits short of graduating because he embarked on a hockey career that was halted by a knee injury. But he had his auctioneer's license at eighteen, and he was working heavy equipment[5], driving a brand new pick-up, and banking good money—all before he was twenty! Before he was thirty, he had a short stint as a roughneck on an oil rig until injured on the job, he had established himself as an award-winning car salesmen, he had two of his own businesses, had built two houses, had three kids, and added general and life-insurance agent and real-estate agent to his list of accomplishments. All the while, he was raising me. Terry became not only my lover and friend, but also a teacher, motivator, father figure, and protector. He encouraged me to try to do things on my own, and sometimes I would be frustrated and angry.

At times I felt tormented and verbally and emotionally abused. We had some nasty fights. There were times he wanted to leave, or I did—but we stuck it out. I can't believe how hard it must have been for a young man trying to be all those things and not having any experience at any of it, just doing the best he could out of love for me. He made some mistakes but was always devoted to me—and I was high-maintenance: not easy to live with and not appreciative at the time of the energy he put into our relationship, providing for us all at the same time. Through all the years, there are still times when we get on each other's nerves and say things that hurt and that we wish we could take back. But more and more, every day, we grow closer and deeper in love. Love, true love, is unconditional. It doesn't mean we have to agree all the time or even that we need to like each other all the time. What it means is that we can express ourselves and our opinions and know that, no matter what, our love is always there, unwavering, steadfast, and true. Tragedy can tear people apart or bring them

---

5   Terry worked at a pulp and paper mill, operating a Laterno, a massive machine that could pick up an entire truckload of logs with one grasp of its huge tongs.

together. We have lived with adversity. Our life together has been one challenge after another. This has given us what we needed to pull together time and again. And through it all Terry's family has been there.

The Atkinsons took me in even before Terry and I were married. I lived in their home and shared a room with Terry's younger sister, Lorraine. Patsy, Terry's oldest sister, was married and lived a few miles away. Her husband, Bob Weir, ran the general store, and they lived in a mobile home just behind it. There was a home attached to the store and a few years later, when Bob's Mom moved out, Bob and Patsy moved in. Carolyn, the first of Bob and Patsy's two girls, was born when I first entered their lives. Roy, Terry's older brother, was getting married to Bob's sister, Jackie. They all taught me a lot, not least that I needed to pitch in and work if I was going to be part of the family. Not really ever having had to work before, and not knowing how to cook, I did a lot of work and spent a lot of years before finally getting the hang of it. I think I've only recently caught on!

That was not just a challenge for me; I think the Atkinsons had a bigger challenge in trying to teach me things I should have already known. All I had ever been responsible for, living with my parents, was tidying my room, and I couldn't even do that right! All at once I'm on a farm. There are chores and housework to do, and each season brought a myriad of new lessons. I learned about calving, pigging, chickens, butchering, feeding, medicating, and doctoring animals. There were mornings I'd get up to catch the school bus and have to step over a new calf lying on the porch. Sometimes I'd be wakened on a cold winter night to help run boxes of newborn pigs to the warmth of the house from the pig barn. It seemed as if animals always picked nights when it was about forty degrees below zero to give birth! Terry's Mom, Vi, taught me how to separate milk and clean the cursed separator. She taught me to cook and keep house. All the while they reinforced for me that patience, love, and acceptance were what was required to be a family that worked together and looked after one another. They never made me feel like an outsider. They became my family, and if I told them thank you every day for the rest of my life I could never come close to expressing the gratitude and love I have for them all.

CHAPTER THREE
They Say Time Heals

I've learned that love, not time,
heals all wounds.

—ANDY ROONEY

Time Heals. How often have you heard that? It is something people say when they are trying to comfort you in your grief and
they don't know what else to say. That's okay. It is wonderful that
people try to help you even if they are uncomfortable, even if they
don't understand. Thank God they don't understand, because if they
did they would have to endure the kind of pain we feel. Bless their
hearts. I am grateful and appreciate every remark someone shares with
me, even if I disagree with the comment—like "Time Heals". My
daughter Erin wrote, "I say, time heals wounds of the flesh, but
wounds of the soul will always be felt, year after year." I knew we
thought alike in many things, but sometimes it still surprises me. We
both believe that what time does do, however, is provide us with the
ability to cope with the pain we've endured.

At first it is debilitating, whether you have lost a loved one and have
a wound in your heart and soul, or whether you have a gaping bleeding wound across your face or have injured your back. Such injuries
are obvious to everyone who sees you; you can't hide them. Over
time, however, a bodily wound heals, although there may always be a
visible scar. But the wounded spirit just learns to cope. You adjust, learn
to live with it—or you don't. Coping is an individual thing. How we
deal with pain is unique to each of us. We can't be slotted into a stereo-
type or compared with someone else. If you think someone should be

feeling a certain way two months after losing a loved one—because that is what you were feeling—then you need to think again. That someone is not you.

I learned as a nurse that pain is whatever the person tells you it is. When someone is in pain, emotionally or physically, the pain is real and intense. Pain tolerance varies from individual to individual. What I find to be intense pain, someone else might find only irritating. Remember, my reality is different from yours. Pain is as painful as we feel it to be. It is real.

Imagine someone racked with physical pain from, for example, arthritis. The pain is so intense at first that they find it difficult to move. The pain is always there. The only way they can get through the day is with medication and other treatments such as application of cold or heat, physiotherapy, or diet. As time goes on, however, the pain doesn't change, but people afflicted learn to function in daily life, and people who have never met them before would never guess that they live with that kind of pain. This is the life many people with chronic pain cope with. The body and mind have learned that this pain is normal for them. They have got used to it. Now they may need medication only if the pain spikes—as it may from time to time. Now apply this to someone who has lost a precious loved one. I have noticed that no matter the loss or the extent of anguish, the devastation is numbing and paralysing at first. Time helps you cope.

I believe that each person's pain is devastating for them and should never be compared with someone else's, but I have heard that there are losses that count as the three most devastating losses of all. They are (in random order):

• Loss of a parent as a child;
• Loss of a spouse or life partner;
• Loss of a child.

Thankfully, I don't know what it is like to lose a spouse. But having lost both parents when I was barely eighteen, and having lost an eighteen-year-old daughter, I know that both these take you to a depth of anguish that cannot even be imagined because it is so raw, biting and hideous it leaves you breathless. I have to say, though, that losing our dear Jessie Jean was the worst, most unbearable, indescribable, life-threatening grief. It is as if something reaches into your chest and tears a chunk right out of your heart. This wound will never heal, and learning to cope with it will take a lot of time.

I have seen parents grieving and coping with the loss of a child to suicide and parents who have lost a child or children to illness or trauma. One thing seems to linger in the wounded hearts of the suicide-stricken parents like a poison, aggravating the grief to a point where coping, for some, may not be possible as long as it exists. This poison is guilt.

We all experience those "woulda, shoulda, couldas", those "what ifs" and "If onlys". When a child dies by suicide, blame, regret, and guilt swell up like an abscess ready to burst and infect our entire life—our entire world—until we are so sickened by it that we stop living. I have also noticed that, just when everyone around you seems to be coping well, some of us don't feel we are there yet. This often comes about two years after the loss, as I mentioned earlier. This also seems to happen to the nurturer of the family. When everyone else is okay, and you don't have to worry any more about anyone else, it's your turn to sink for a while. Besides, two years feels like only a few months in "grief time." Don't think you aren't coping; you are just doing it on your terms.

CHAPTER FOUR

Coping

G uilt, that horrible abscess, will drag you into a bottomless pit of despair. To survive, you must do something that takes a lot of courage—face your guilt head-on, acknowledge its poison, and lance it like a boil. One quick, painful stroke, saying out loud:

> "I will not feel guilty any more.
> This was not about me; it is not my fault."

Believe it, because it is true. I know of parents racked with guilt because their last words to their child were words of anger and they have no parting note, no way of knowing what their offspring was feeling or thinking when the child took his or her last breath. I'm sure they have treated others as they did that child, said similar things to other members of their family—yet those family members are still alive. Believe that your tragedy is not your fault; get rid of the poisonous guilt before it's too late. It takes courage and willpower to conquer guilt, but it *must* be done. Allow yourself to live again. See the joy in life within you and all around you. Save yourself. I see parents with other children, grandchildren, and extended families who stop appreciating the wonder of the lives around them. Struck deaf and blind by guilt, they no longer recognize their many blessings.

What is that doing to the rest of the family? They have already lost one person they love to suicide; now they are losing another to an infection of the soul. Why wallow in the darkness? What's the point of wilfully committing suicide of the spirit? You must do whatever it takes—make it your mission, a quest—to find joy, to hold on to it like a life preserver, and to learn to live again.

It is in you to do this. If you don't have the strength to do it alone, find someone, or something, to help you. You will find it. It may be in nature, in meditation, in faith, or in prayer. It may be the life of a newborn baby; it may be a milestone for a child in your life who needs you to share in the celebration. Release the guilt and allow the light to dance into your heart once again. You deserve to live, to love, and to laugh—and those close to you need you back, living and loving and laughing in their world, too.

Something to think about: Many people who have attempted suicide tell us that they believed the people they love would be better off without them. They wanted to die so that they wouldn't be a bother any more. They felt they were a source of pain and stress on their families. Of course, they are wrong, but at the moment they lashed out at themselves, the last thing they wanted to do was hurt *us*. The furthest thing from their thoughts was to make us miserable for the rest of our lives. Most often it is the opposite: they want us to be happy, especially since they couldn't find happiness themselves.

Our circumstances were different. I have few regrets. Terry carries more guilt than I for reasons he can best explain. Jessie and I said "I Love You" to each other as some of the last words we spoke.

She left a note for Erin and an audio tape, talking in turn to Terry and me; our son, Clint, and our daughter, Erin; Jessie's friends, Raemona Smith, Dustin Jones (DJ), and Nathan Lamoureux; and then to all her other friends (she tried naming them all) and to her extended family. We know that her heart was full of love for us. She told us that it had nothing to do with us and that she knew she was loved. It was all about her and her inability to suffer one more day. She couldn't take the emotional pain of depression anymore. This tape was yet another gift to help us deal with this tragedy.

If you fell out of a boat in the ocean, would you close your eyes and simply sink into the depths, or would you fight to keep your head above water and swim hard for the life ring thrown out to you? Many people are throwing you lifelines; you just need to reach for one and hang on, kick hard and fight to keep breathing. They will help to pull you back aboard.

(If you said to yourself, "I'd sink," when you read this, please consider going to Appendix "H" right now to read about the signs and symptoms of depression and the resources available to help you through your pain. Some mild depression symptoms are quite normal when we grieve, but when a part of you wants to die, it is time to seek some experienced help.)

Thank God I am blessed with the gifts I have been given to get me through this. There are so many, it would take a library of books to list them all. I am thankful for my family, my amazing friends, my spiritual journey. But I am also thankful for everything we take for granted. I'm grateful for the air I breathe; for good health and the ability to take each breath without effort or pain; for being able to read. I am thankful that my parents loved me, that I live in a country where no bombs are dropping and no landmines litter the countryside, and that I have loose change in my pocket for trivial things like a bag of treats to nibble on while I watch TV or work at my computer. How blessed am I? Amazingly blessed!

Being able to be thankful is the first major step in coping. You have heard "count your blessings" before, but have you done it lately? If not, put this book down and start looking around you. Look in a mirror. Do you have a roof over your head, food in your kitchen, and clothes on your back? Look in your closets, look at photo albums, look out your window. Aren't you blessed that you have a window? Take it all in. Do you see how much you have? Now say out loud to the universe or whatever deity or creator you believe in, "Thank You." If you can't do this right now—if you aren't in the right place emotionally—I would ask that you try it anyway. Do it again tomorrow morning before you even get out of bed. Try a bit every day, and soon your days will look better and better. No more helpful words were ever spoken than "count your blessings". No matter what life throws at you, there are many things to be thankful for, and these blessings are the lines that tether us and keep us from being blown, tossed and swallowed up by the storm of life. Hang on to them, your blessings.

Be thankful that you recognize them and understand—no, *know*—that you are blessed. Not in spite of all you have endured, but *because* of it.

Every experience changes us somehow. Sometimes it's a joyful event; other times it's a challenge we must struggle through to grow and learn. But sometimes we must endure pain. We experience an event so traumatic that it damages us. The damage is evident, a constant reminder of the event that caused it. Memory keeps the wound open and raw. How we perceive each experience and how we cope with it are important to our survival and health. Terry and I learned that there is a reason that he would feel especially down on the same day I would be particularly strong and happy, or I was down and he was "up." It was so that we could help each other through. It took us a while to figure it out. When I was really blue, I would be cranky and miserable, but I didn't want to tell Terry I was sad because I didn't want to ruin his good day! News Flash! I was ruining it anyway by being so hard to live with! Once we promised to tell each other when we were especially blue, our relationship got stronger. We were able to accept help when we needed it and we felt great being able to give the help when we were able. We never know what will trigger a spell of weeping and feeling blue. It might be a song on the radio or a drive through the countryside. For example, I can't look at plums in the grocery store without tears (you'll read about why later in the book). But then there are special days: birthdays, holidays, and any day that is significant in the life of the loved one we have lost. In the Introduction, I told of the Candle Light Service presented by a funeral home as a way to help people handle loss during the Christmas season. On Jessie's birthday, we have an ice-cream cake, and perhaps a few of Jessie's friends come over. But let me share another idea on how to get through the "worse" days. One of those days I call the Perennial day.

PERENNIAL DAY?

My Parents' is June 27th. Jessie's is May 25th. Sometimes the day of the week at the time of year is worse than the actual date. The Thursday before the Grande Prairie Regional High School's graduation celebrations—that's when Jessie died. I always thought it was weird and cumbersome calling this day "The anniversary of her death". I think of anniversaries as being an annual day of celebrating a happy event like a wedding. So I thought about what else comes every year. Plants. I love perennials; they are so easy to look after. My garden is full of them. I thought, perennials come back every year; they are something beautiful that grows out of the cold, dark depths. They appear to die in the winter and are reborn into a new life again in the spring. That sounded like the perfect word to use.

JESSIE'S PERENNIAL DAY

How does anyone get through that day? What should you do? It's approaching and you're thinking about it; it weighs on you and distracts you, creates anxiety, freshens the sense of loss. You miss your loved one immensely. You may get irritable, or weepy, or both. But guess what? You aren't alone. Everyone who feels the loss is going through the same thing, quietly, privately. I remember that after Jessie's memorial service following her funeral, the family and some close friends went to Cliff and Lorraine Rule's (Terry's sister's home). We had supper and wound down there in the company of those closest to us. Jessie's friends didn't want to intrude; they would have felt out of place. But they, too, needed more reflection and winding-down time. So we told them to head over to our house, start up the bonfire and make themselves at home. They knew the few rules and requests we have, and we felt comfortable allowing them to be there while we weren't at home. When we finally did get home, a wake was in full swing. Spending time with those kids was so renewing. They energize us and make us feel young, loved and needed—full of purpose. We were there for each other. I don't know whether they all understand how much they have done for us by just being there. The support of our friends and family have been our source of strength—giving us what we need to go on. That support came not just from our own friends, but from our children's friends and some of their parents as well.

A year was almost past. May 25th was right around the corner. We knew we weren't the only ones feeling out of sorts, so we invited friends to join us around the bonfire. I set out Jessie's ball cap (which she liked to wear around the fire pit), a montage of pictures of her, a little poem one of her friends gave us that seemed appropriate, and a small bottle of R&R Whiskey, Jessie's drink.

The kids started coming about 9 p.m., and the party began—laughing and sharing stories, having fun, and remembering Jessie. It was a celebration of life and friendship. It was an especially hard night for DJ, as we learned just how much he loved her and how devastated he was by her loss. That night was the first time I heard Clint speak of that terrible day he found his sister. He was liquored up and it was four in the morning before he began sharing, but I found comfort in the way he spoke, for I could tell he had spoken of it several times before. I knew then for sure that he would be okay. This night was exactly what we all needed. Some drank a little too much, I think in part because it serves as a way to loosen inhibitions and allows them to share deep feelings with us and others. Perhaps, too, because that is what kids do at a party—part of their social activities, a comfort zone. But it was also because they knew they were safe. I don't drink, so I made sure that they had food to eat and a place to sleep. I was told once that they enjoyed our company, even though we were "parents," because we accepted them without passing judgments or preaching. (That was one of the best compliments I have ever received.) The party lasted all night. I went to bed just after four, but Terry stayed up 'til about six. I got up about seven-thirty to make sure the kids who needed to go to work got up in time. I cleaned up the bottles, cans, and leftover food on the tables and around the fire pit, then went in to cook breakfast. My breakfasts were a legend from the morning after the "wake" the year before. As kids got mobile, I fed them. One by one they said their thanks and goodbyes until we were once again alone. We are always sad when the last one leaves. We so enjoy having them around us that we never want it to end. It sounds like a lot of work for me, but it doesn't feel like it. I find so much energy in pampering and fussing over my kids.

In May 2002, the kids decided to swim in the dugout. It's all of three feet deep at its centre and contains mostly mud, cattails, weeds, snails, and leeches. It's not what anyone would call a swimming hole, but sometime between four and seven in the morning it must have sounded like a good idea. Someone shouted, "Hey! Can you swim in your dugout?" It must have been a rhetorical question, for before any-one could respond, we heard a loud splash followed by an exuberant cheer in the darkness. Soon the party had moved to the slippery shores of Goose Poop Wallow! When I came out to clean up at seven-thirty, there were muddy clothes, shoes, belts, wallets, soggy cigarettes and money lying in heaps everywhere. I started doing laundry. After breakfast I informed the kids, all dressed in either Erin's clothes or Clint's, that all their own clothes were washed, dried and folded in piles. Belts, wallets and money were assembled for them to claim. More memories made, more fun, and I felt great babying my kids. It was another wonderful day that could have otherwise been lonely, anxious, and sad if we hadn't chosen to share it this way.

May 25th fell on a Sunday in 2003, so we told the kids Saturday night would be the party night. Terry told me not to be too disap-pointed if not many came, as they were growing up, moving away, and getting on with their lives, as young adults do. He had made plans with Clint to go to a "So You Think You're Tough" fight night in Horse Lake (close to Hythe). They would join us later. The kids started arriving one by one and in small groups of friends. Raemona had moved to southern Alberta and couldn't make it, so she phoned and we had a great visit. New kids came. One had lost his brother to suicide in the fall of 1998; another had lost an Uncle to suicide just be-fore Christmas 2002. They came with some of their friends. Our circle widens. During the partying and craziness and carrying on, individuals or small groups of kids wanting to talk seriously would approach Terry or me. We'd have our chats with them and were usually thanked with a hug. On Sunday morning, Danielle Dreger (another of Jessie's friends unable to attend the gathering) phoned. There were kids sleep-ing in the house and in our holiday trailer. Around the fire pit were two never-say-die guys, "Woody" and Jordan. They were just "ex-amining the backs of their eyelids" when I came out to clean up around the fire pit only to find that they had already cleaned up the party mess. What a treat!

I made breakfast in waves as the kids woke up, wandered upstairs and emerged from rooms. After breakfast, some left and some stayed, going out to the fire pit and getting into the beer again. Oh to be young! "Only if you plan on staying longer or you have a ride home,"

I heard myself preach. They knew we would drive them home if needed, but they would never ask that. They had all intended on hanging out with us for the day.

DJ was up from his new home and job in Lethbridge to be at his brother's graduation and to be with us. He laughed as he remembered seeing me help kids find a place to sleep. "And there was Faris," he said," passing out buckets like they were complimentary mints!" Some of those kids hadn't been with us overnight before and they were pretty intoxicated. I wasn't sure how they would react and I didn't want any messes on my carpeting! I had made little nests on couches and beds, and laid extra mattresses on the floor. I had placed drinking water and barf buckets within reach or next to each young face. I checked on them from time to time. Some had brought their own sleeping bags and pillows. "We are definitely coming back again!" said the last of the group leaving about two-thirty Sunday afternoon. "We'll be here next year for sure!" There had been seven left around the campfire at noon, so I had taken out a big vat of Chilli and veggie sticks.

They say you reach a man's heart through his stomach, Well, I keep my kids hanging around just a little longer by feeding them, but their hearts were touched long before food was even mentioned. They came for us, for themselves, for their friends, and for Jessie. They stayed because they know we love them and they feel good when they are with us. We all feel loved: no judgments, no conditions, just love and acceptance. For a short while they feel safe being who they are and sharing a deep part of themselves with parental figures that aren't their parents, so they can be friends too. I remember opening the door to my home one day to see a guy standing there with a shaved head, wearing black, laden with chains, sporting army boots, and multiple piercings and tattoos. If I had made a judgment on him by his appearance at that time, I would have deprived myself of knowing a wonderful young man.

Things that stood out for me this year were the spontaneous acts of sincere appreciation for Terry and me. For me, it was when "Woody" (Dean Smith, Raemona's brother) held his drink in the air and started to chant. Soon more joined in. I'll never forget it, the kids all holding their drinks in the air shouting, "We love Faris, We Love Faris" I cried. I witnessed their feelings for Terry too. Remember, Terry and Clint had gone to a sporting event earlier in the evening. The kids kept asking, "Where's Terry? When's Terry gonna be here?" When he came, they all got up and rushed over to greet him with hugs and handshakes, honestly pleased to see him and glad he was finally there. They gathered around him like a returning hero. The love, respect, and appreciation these remarkable young people show is sincere. It's straight from the heart and we are blessed to receive it. When they have all gone home, Terry and I sit together silently; we can't wait till they all come back again.

This is Jessie's Perennial day and this is how we have chosen to acknowledge it. Now, instead of a day we dread, it's a day we plan for with joy. We have turned it around and built happiness from sorrow.

CHAPTER FIVE

Grandpa and Granny

GRANDPA

We called Terry's father "Dad" until the grandkids started arriving, and then it was "Grandpa". The first granddaughter lovingly called him Popeye, and my siblings continued that endearment. Friends and family called him Allan—his given name—or, more commonly, "Doc." He was probably best known as Doc or Uncle Doc. He got the name during World War II. He came from a large family and he was one of the youngest boys. His older brothers went to Edmonton to join up and told him to stay home. Instead, he lied about his age and joined up in Calgary so his brothers wouldn't know. He was sixteen, seventeen when he landed in Europe. His brothers didn't find out until after VE Day when he was standing in line to sign up for the fighting in the Pacific and one of his brothers, Sam, spotted him. What a reunion that must have been! He never spoke much of the war and never watched war movies; it was too painful. However, if pressed, he might speak of some of the fun or funny events that occurred from time to time. His buddies named him "Doc" from Bugs Bunny's famous opening greeting—"What's up Doc?" The horrors he must have witnessed and been part of can only be imagined, never understood by those of us who weren't there. I remember hearing him screaming profanities and threats while he slept. His nightmares haunted him all the years after the war. He wouldn't attend Remembrance Day ceremonies on November 11. He preferred to go out in the bush on that day. He loved to hunt, walking silently through the bush, listening to nature and beholding its glory. This was one place where he felt at peace.

I knew Doc to be a quiet, sweet, and gentle man. He loved his family and worried about them incessantly. I didn't know him when he was younger, when he was working in logging and construction camps, unable to spend much time with his family and struggling with alcoholism. I met him after all that. I learned that he attended one Alcoholics Anonymous meeting and quit drinking on his own. It takes a very brave person even to recognize that he or she has a problem—to beat it is astounding; I have great respect for people who can do that. But to do it on your own is miraculous! When we first met, he loved me right away. We spent a lot of time together, talking and working, and he taught me a great deal. I know I must have been a real handful. I had moved out to Terry's home about a year after losing my parents, sharing a room with Terry's younger sister, Lorraine, next to Vi and Doc's room. Terry and Roy slept in a room across the hall. Patsy, Terry's oldest sibling, had once shared a room with her sister, but married a few years earlier and had a baby girl with one on the way. Her husband, Bob Weir, and his Mom ran the Goodfare Store a few miles away. Patsy and Bob had a mobile home just behind the store. Roy moved out when he married Jackie, Bob's sister, in 1975. They had a home just a couple of miles south of Vi and Doc's.

I'll never forget Grandpa's compassion and empathy for me. He never scolded me, raised his voice, or got mad at me. I caught hell from Granny a few times when I wasn't towing the line, and I got in a few scraps with Lorraine and Patsy, but I never felt as if I was not part of the family. Although he never got mad at me, Grandpa sure liked to tease. He would take special joy in pacing back and forth behind me and whomever I was working with while we stood at the kitchen sink doing dishes. His wool socks would have been pulled half way off his feet when he removed his gumboots to come into the house after doing chores, and the toe ends would flop ahead of his feet as he walked. His eyes would sparkle and he'd speak with a broad smile and a lilt in his voice, chiming, "Oh, look how happy you are doing dishes. I can see you smiling; I can tell how much you love to scrub those pots." On and on he'd go. At times I wanted to lash out and tell him to get off our backs, but then it became an irritating game. Now I wish I could hear him tease me again, if only one last time.

One summer, everyone had a job or was in school except for Grandpa and me. The hay needed to be put up, so I was asked to give Grandpa a hand. I had helped with chores, so I knew how to handle bales and knew they were heavy, but I had never been out on the sloop behind the baler putting up stooks before! I was taught. We started early with a breakfast of fried potatoes, back bacon or pork chops, toast, eggs and tea. After breakfast, lunch was packed, tea put in the thermos, and water jugs filled. We sat drinking our tea while we had a smoke and rolled more for the day. Grandpa told me that I'd have "muscles in my shit" by the time the summer was out, and I laughed as we packed up the smokes, cleaned up the loose tobacco on the table, put away the papers, and got ready to hit the fields. I had no experience driving a tractor, let alone while pulling a square baler with a sloop dragging behind that. So I was the stooker. It was hot and dusty, but I had to wear long sleeves, jeans, and boots to keep from getting scratched up. I also wore leather gloves and a leather apron with straps to tie part of the apron around each leg, almost like a short pair of chaps. The bales weighed an average of 65 to 70 pounds of dried grasses (timothy, alfalfa and brome), sweet clover, and the odd wild rose bush. It was prickly and heavy and, hot as I was, I was thankful for the protective clothing. It was hard work. I ate like a king, slept like a baby and could look back on a field with a huge sense of accomplishment because I could see what we had done. At the end of the season, we put up straw bales. They weighed about 10 to 20 pounds each and felt like air to stook. Grandpa was right. I think I had built up muscles in places I didn't know muscles were. I would be out there standing on the sloop, sweat dripping off my nose and burning my eyes, dust and chaff sticking to my face. I'd grab a bale by the twine and fling it between the rods to start the bottom row. One after another would hammer out of the baler and be thrown into place. The last bale sits on top of the triangular stack to complete the stook. I'd use my leg to give it the extra boost I needed to fling it over my head and set it atop the pyramid. Then I'd step on the release lever that lowered the rods to the ground, put a well placed shoulder to the stack, and gently nudge it off the sloop in time to grab the next bale and start all over again.

Grandpa felt bad and got me to drive the tractor for a while, but I'd leave so much of the swath behind when I took a corner, we'd have to go back around the field again to pick up all the missed hay. I told him I really didn't mind the physical work, and honestly, I just didn't feel right having him do that strenuous work. One of the best summers I can remember was that one, and those long hours working with him.

Grandpa had three heart attacks. The first was pretty major and landed him in intensive care for several days. We thought we were going to lose him. That was 1979. But he was one of the strongest people I have ever known—not just spiritually, but physically as well. That seems to be an Atkinson trait, surprising physical strength for their size. They all have it and it never ceases to amaze me. So Grandpa survived. He recovered fully and quit smoking, but his eating habits never changed much. Years later, when he was suffering with digestive problems, he ate antacid tablets like candy. He started feeling down all the time and complained a lot. This went on for so long, it seemed as if this was his new nature—a whiner. Eventually, he was diagnosed with a hiatus hernia and gallbladder problems. They had him in for surgery to repair the hernia and remove the gallbladder. When surgeons went in they were surprised to find his gallbladder so shrivelled and full of infection that they opted not to do the hernia repair they had intended. They were shocked. Gangrene in his gallbladder—how could anyone have coped with that kind of pain? No one they had ever heard of had had this kind of infection there before. The pain a patient would be experiencing would have led him to do something about the gallbladder long before an infection of this kind could develop. Most people would have collapsed in agony, even lost consciousness, long before this stage. Not Grandpa. He just appeared to be "not well" and had been labelled a "whiner". A whiner? I don't think so!

His last heart attack was mild compared to the first. I was working as an emergency medical technician (EMT-A) with the Beaverlodge-Hythe Ambulance service at the time. It was the last day of school in June. Granny Vi was the first woman to drive school bus for the County of Grande Prairie, and she drove for just over thirty years. On this day, after dropping the kids home, Granny took her bus into

Grande Prairie to the County Shop for the summer. She was catching a ride home with someone, so Grandpa was at home on their farm in Goodfare, a small farming community about an hour west of Grande Prairie. The two had spent a good part of the day in the garden before bus time and Grandpa was tired.

It must have been five or six when Grandpa called our home to talk to Terry. We lived a half-hour from Goodfare, right in Beaverlodge where Terry had an insurance and real estate business. Terry wasn't home from work yet. Grandpa was just wondering if Terry could come and pick him up and bring him into town. I told him to give Terry a call at his office and hung up. Soon I started to worry. It didn't make sense. I started asking myself questions right away. Why?

Grandpa had his own means of getting into town, and he usually didn't make the trip unless he really needed to. Why call Terry to get him? This was so out of character; alarm bells started ringing in my head. I knew something was wrong. I phoned him back. After the "hello"s, our conversation went something like this:

"What's wrong?"

"I just don't feel well," Grandpa said.

"What do you mean—how don't you feel well?" I could hear him breathing quite quickly into the phone, as if he were out of breath.

"Mostly upset stomach is all; must've been something I ate at lunch"

"What were you doing before you started feeling bad?" I asked.

'Working in the garden, so I came in and lay down for a while."

"Are you having any chest pain?"

"Well, I guess maybe a little bit," Grandpa replied.

"You know what I think it is? You know, too, don't you?"

"Yeah, but . . . ."

I asked if he had taken any nitroglycerin, and he said he had.

"How much? One dose? Two? Three?"

Grandpa said he had taken three.

"And you still feel bad? Grandpa, listen to me, you know what I think we should do. I'm calling the ambulance."

Grandpa protested: "Now you don't have to go and do that."

But I insisted: "Yes, I do. Now listen, you lie down."

"It hurts to lie down."

"Prop yourself up on the couch with your feet up then, and do not move for anything until we get there. Okay? Promise?"

"Okay"

I hung up and called Gary Rycroft. Gary and I had gone to high school together; now he owned and operated the ambulance service. He wasn't just a friend, but my boss too.

Gary said he would pick Grandpa up and that Bruce Wideman would go with him. Bruce was the person I partnered with most on the ambulance. Then Gary asked if I wanted to come.

"Yes!" I said. "I'll meet you at the fire hall in a few minutes!"

Terry was already on his way to his dad's. I called Grandpa back.

"Grandpa," I told him, "the ambulance is on its way and Terry should be there soon. I thought I told you not to move. That means do not get up and answer the phone. Do you understand? If the phone rings again, don't answer the damn thing!"

"OK," he replied softly. I was out the door and gone. I was glad I was there for him as a daughter and as a health-care professional. He recovered yet again. He seemed invincible.

Oh the memories! We have memories of camping, quading (riding all-terrain vehicles), and fishing with the whole family. Thanks to

Camping in the Rocky Mountains by Red Deer Falls, close to Tumbler Ridge B.C.

Quadding in to Onion Lake. View of Wapiti Lake, Rocky Mountains, B.C. From left: Cody Dunbar, Clint (son) and Joe Atkinson (nephew). (Picture taken by Dillon Rule – nephew)

video cameras, we have a lot of these memories on tape. Thank God for those extra years, because then the cancer came. By the time he finally went to the doctor about his difficulty urinating, the prostate cancer had metastasized into his bones. He would have two years, one good and one not so good. As time went by, he went from a rotund, active, independent man to a frail, thin, bed-ridden one, relying on family and nursing care to provide for him. Granny kept him at home for as long as she could, right until almost the very end. He went into hospital several days before he died. One day two years earlier, Grandpa and I were looking through music and listening to songs. I was trying to find something appropriate to sing at a friend's funeral. Grandpa told me he wanted me to sing at his funeral service and told me what song he wanted. I didn't want to think about it at the time, but I'm glad I listened to his wishes.

Time passed. It was October 1992. We spent hours at the hospital, and we all had an opportunity to tell Grandpa how much we loved him. I don't know what finally killed him, the cancer or the high doses of morphine needed to manage the pain. There were times when we sat at his bedside and heard him mutter delusions induced by his medications.

It was sad and funny, sometimes all at once. One day he was speaking to an old friend, Jack, at the foot of the bed. The conversation was two-way, but Grandpa was the only one who could see or hear Jack, who had passed away years before. The way Grandpa interacted with this apparition was so real and seemingly lucid, it made us wonder—maybe it was real. Who's to say? It was real enough to Grandpa, and isn't that the most important thing?

It was hard on everyone watching Grandpa die, seeing this proud man with his dignity so compromised. Grandpa was a loving, generous, and caring man, always worried about the ones he loved, always wanting to keep us all from harm, and it was hard to see him suffer that long, torturous death. We spent hours with him and with each other, riddled with bouts of guilt, shame, and feelings of selfishness for momentary lapses of wishing he'd just go. It was painful for all of us, not just Grandpa.

I felt he held his dignity to the end, brave, strong, and wonderful. I never heard of anyone going through "dying breaths" (Cheyne-Stokes respirations) for longer than a few hours before death. Grandpa did it for almost three days! This is the hardest time of all: a deep breath followed by a shallower one and a shallower one until they are so shallow there is no breath, nothing—ten seconds, fifteen seconds, still no breath, twenty seconds. He must be gone; we are about to start to grieve—and then, all at once, a long, slow, deep breath followed by a shallower one, and the cycle would start all over again.

I can't imagine the physical pain Grandpa had to endure, or the psychological anguish of waiting for death to come. But I was a part of the pain this wonderful family had to experience, being with him and watching helpless as he slipped away from this world.

It was hard at the time to see the blessings and joys that came out of this traumatic loss. I could, because I had lost my parents those many years before and had learned from it. I saw a close family draw closer. I saw sons—men who hadn't been comfortable hugging their father or saying "I love you" to him out loud—able to exchange these intimacies at his deathbed. If he had died of his first heart attack in 1979, they would never have got the chance. I saw the family learn how to appreciate life and each other as never before. Having gone through this experience, they were able to help others through similar times, offering what they knew would help because it was what they needed during their own time of mourning. This event sent Terry down a path of discovery that he might otherwise never have taken. He became a man on a mission, determined to find out more about health and treatments and alternatives to conventional medicine. He became an insatiable student, reading and learning everything he could. He continues his quest today. He has helped other people with cancer find new directions when conventional medicine has let them down or given up on them. He has literally saved lives from what he has learned, spurred on by his quest for knowledge and answers to his questions about why Dad had to die that way.

Grandpa was special to all his grandkids, and they all love him like no other. He made such an impression on them that they continue to remember, imitate, emulate, and talk about him to this day, even though some of his grandkids have lived longer without him than with him. Some of them have told about Grandpa's spirit visiting them when they were at low points in their lives, usually when they were afraid. They felt him near and felt his strength nourish them and give them what they needed to get through that hard time. Jessie was especially close to Grandpa; they seemed kindred spirits. She missed him greatly, spoke of him often, and would visit his gravesite regularly. She placed a lock of her hair under an ornament on his grave because he loved her long hair so much. He used to sing to her, "Jessie Jean, my little Queen, with eyes so bluish green and a 1982 spleen." She would beam. She wrote about him and to him after he died.

One day Jessie shared with Terry and me a dream she had: she was climbing a mountain, working hard at climbing the rocks and cliffs, slipping back, feeling tired and frustrated. But she kept going until she finally reached the top. When she pulled herself up on the summit, the peak was like a large meadow that stretched out before her. Grandpa was walking toward her. He was his big, round, smiling self, wearing a T-shirt and jacket, jeans, and gumboots not on all the way (he used to "walk into" his boots). But he wasn't wearing glasses. She was immensely please to see him and he her.

They hugged. She asked him why he wasn't wearing his glasses, and he told her that you don't need glasses in heaven. They stood together, arms around each other, and looked at the view. "Isn't it beautiful?"

he asked her. "This could all be yours", he added, "so quit pissing around!"

After sharing this dream with us, Jessie said it didn't feel like a dream; it had felt real. What could it all mean? Not having read or learned anything on dream interpretation, we just discussed it together and gave our ideas.

"Well,' we said, "you never gave up climbing the mountain even though it was hard and you got knocked back a few times. You felt good about that when you finally got to the top. Maybe there is a lesson for you there. Maybe the message is that you shouldn't give up, that it's all worth the effort in the end."

We told her that maybe she didn't dream about Grandpa—maybe he visited her in her dream. Maybe Grandpa was trying to tell her to stay focused, not go off track, and she'll be able to reach her goals. Terry and I suggested that this referred to her schoolwork and graduating. In retrospect, I think she interpreted it altogether differently. He was in her last thoughts as she left this world. In the audiotape she left us, her last words were a little giggle and "Don't worry about me; I'll be with Grandpa". We buried her ashes next to his in the cemetery that she had visited so often. She is with him in this world and the next.

GRANNY VI

I could write a chapter on each person who has influenced me in some way and their connection to me, but I feel that I *need* to tell you about this special person in my life, as she has had an enormous influence on whom I have become.

Her whole life, Viola Atkinson worked hard and cared for others. She stood by her husband when he suffered through alcoholism, and she gave him the incentive, motivation, and strength he needed to help him conquer that demon. She raised her four children and, from time to time, other people's children, myself included. And all this while Allan (Grandpa or Doc) was working away from home most of the time. But she didn't just stay home milking cows, gardening, canning preserves, running the farm, raising chickens, pigs and cattle—all on top of keeping house and looking after kids. She did it all in a home that, for a time, had a wood stove for heat and didn't include such amenities as the washing machines and dishwashers we have now. Besides this, she drove school bus for more than thirty years. Over the years, Vi worked as a café manager and chef, as a runner in the provincial courthouse and as a matron at the jail, among other things. She is no stranger to work and still finds or makes work to keep herself busy every day. She looked after her mom when she was ill, and she tended to Doc as his health declined. She made and kept strong friendships in the community and has been active in many organizations such as Rural Crime Watch, the Goodfare Hall Board, and many others. Vi is a well-known and highly respected person. But she does take time to enjoy herself by doing things that relax her. She likes to go camping, fishing and hunting. She enjoys crafts and has recently got quite creative and talented in ceramics. She likes to play the nickel machines at the local casino from time to time, and she loves to curl. She spends most winter weekends in some bonspiel or other. But I think she gets the greatest joy from just being with her family, her kids, grandkids and great grandson. And we get great joy from spending time with her. It seems that she is always "looking after us," and whenever we visit we are well fed—and usually bring home with us a bag of this, a jar or two of that, and a box of something else. She has us call her when we get home so she knows we are safe.

Since Grandpa passed away, Granny has found a new partner, Wilson Will—Uncle Willy. He was married to Allan's sister Tress, who passed away after a long battle with Parkinson's disease. Willy was devoted to her. After both he and Granny had been widowed for some time, their relationship blossomed into more than just old and dear friends and in-laws who had always been there for each other. We are all so happy that they found love together. It is a wonderful thing, to find a long-lasting and loving relationship with a partner, but it is a true and precious blessing to find it twice in the same lifetime.

Vi means a great deal to me. She has the courage of a lion; it seems nothing scares her. She will fight for herself and she will fight for those she loves or those who have no one to fight for them. I feel safe when I'm with her. She has the heart of a bear: when she has her heart set on something, there isn't much that can deflect her from her course. She is steadfast, with amazing strength of character and the tenacity to endure whatever life throws at her—and it has flung a lot her way. I feel inspired by her. She has the wisdom of the ages, and through her life's experiences she has learned a wealth of lessons. I feel like a student with Vi as my mentor. I have learned and continue to learn from her. She has the humility of a lamb and, although her humility may not be obvious to people who don't know her well, I have seen it and it is beautiful. I feel I can share anything with her because she is so approachable. I never feel I need to be anyone or anything other than my true self when I am with her. She has the generosity of a flower, open to share whatever she can offer with whoever needs it. She makes me want to strive to be better than I am. She has a soul overflowing with love. At times, you see the lion or the bear because that is what she needs to be, but her loving spirit is always her guide. Everything she does is led by love.

It has been years since this family became my own. Through all the years, the ups and downs, our love has grown. When Terry and I were first married and we had a tiff, I would run home to *his* mother—and she was always there for me. Losing Jessie was one of the hardest things any one of us had gone through, and yet we drew strength from one another, each helping as we were able and receiving help from others when we needed it. As I reflected on all that the Atkinsons have blessed me with, I began to wonder whether I would ever be able to express equal love for them. They know I love them, but what they have

Viola Atkinson (Granny Vi) & Allan (Doc) Atkinson (Grandpa). This photo was taken in about 1988 when Allan worked as security at the Canadian Air Force Base in Beaverlodge, Alberta.

given me is immeasurable. Raising me was a hard job, and it wasn't something any of them had to do. They just did. Both Doc and Vi taught me much, and they loved me as parents when I wasn't very lovable sometimes. When Grandpa was diagnosed with cancer, we all became closer yet. As he became bedridden, he was cared for at home until the last several days of his life. I remember how Granny confided in me at the hospital as Grandpa was dying. I felt special to be there for her at that moment. I remembered Grandpa telling me he wanted me to sing a certain song for him at his funeral. His faith in me gave me the strength I needed, and I did it. I was so thankful I had the chance to give something back to these amazing people I love so much. But another chance was yet to come.

Granny had faced cancer before: she had been treated for bladder cancer; she had lost a young nephew to it. She had watched her husband die of cancer. Now she was told she had a cancerous lump in her breast. She was given the option of a lumpectomy and being treated with radiation, or having a complete mastectomy. She refused to go through radiation treatments and opted for the mastectomy. This was very upsetting for many members of the family. Her sisters, her two daughters, and two sons were especially affected, I think. Of all her family, who would gladly have stood by her from start to finish, she asked me to be by her side in the hospital. You can only imagine how touched I was, honoured to be "the chosen one". My heart was full and I wept.

The hospital room was crowded with family as she prepared to go "under the knife". But I was the one who went with her into the staging area or prep room just a few steps from the operating rooms. I had my orders; I knew my job. I was to make sure she was looked after properly, that she had what she needed, that everything was questioned and analyzed to ensure her safe and proper care. I was to be her advocate. As we waited for the doctor to visit her just before the surgery, she looked at me with watery eyes and asked, "Do you think I'm doing the right thing?"

Wow. That's pretty powerful. She is asking me? A part of me wanted to cry out, "Don't do it!" but I heard words come out of my mouth that were wise and seemed to be guided from something larger than myself.

"Do you want to put your moccasins on and run for the door?" I asked. She answered me right away: "No."

"Then," I said, "For you, you are doing the right thing." I said a lot of the family thought she was moving too fast and was making a rash decision that she might regret later, but I told her I had the feeling she had been thinking about making this decision for a long time. I believed this wasn't a decision made at the spur of the moment at all, but thought out thoroughly and played out in her mind many times over the years.

She told me I was right and I could see her relax and feel better. I made sure all her questions were asked when the doctor saw her, and I made sure she had answers she understood. I was the last family member she saw before she went to surgery, and the first one she saw when she came back to her room. I did what was asked of me and felt proud to have been able to do it. Finally, I was in some small measure able to give back something in return for the many things she has given me. And I was grateful to have been given the opportunity. She has always made me feel special and loved and like one of her very own. I just hope I have done the same for her. Thanks, Mom.

CHAPTER SIX

Tough breaks

Loss can be more than just loss through death. It can be loss of almost anything, including loosing the sense that a new day is a fresh start and everything will be okay.

Ever had a run of bad luck? Most of us have. They say that luck runs in threes. Maybe so, and maybe it runs in multiples of three. I've lost count, so I can't say. Our family had a nasty run of events that is so unbelievable; we actually lived it and yet we still find it incredible. Sometimes we had to laugh, sometimes cry, sometimes both. Even in the midst of it, we would shake our heads and say to each other with a chuckle, "Can you believe this? What next?" During that time we lost something: the feeling that a certain event can never happen to you, only to someone else. It is the feeling that allows us to step confidently into our day and live life to its fullest, unafraid, secure in the knowledge that we can do what we need to do. Without that ability, we are anxious and looking over our shoulders, focusing on what *might* happen instead of how we can make things happen as we want them to. Like a bird on the ground, we are twitching and nervous, watchful of the dangers that may pounce at any moment. We have lost our liberty because our fears are determining our actions—and all because we lost that blissful sense of being invincible. The events that stripped us of our happy freedom from constant worry started at the end of August 1998 when Clint was back at the Athol Murray College of Notre

Dame. After graduating from Grade 12 at this prestigious private school in June, he was returning to play Tier Two Junior A Hockey with the Notre Dame Hounds. He had played both his Midget years there while taking Grades 11 and 12, and he made a name for himself as the Most Valuable Player for the Midget AAA Hounds the year he graduated. There he was in Wilcox, Saskatchewan, again, but this time it would be a bit different. Not being a high school student there, he would be billeted in a home instead of living in the dorms, and he would be allowed to drive his own vehicle and come and go with more freedom. Clint left his truck with us as it needed to be completely overhauled. It got a new motor, new rear end, and new tires at a total cost of over $16,500—we wanted to make sure it would be reliable on winter roads. It was a sweet, silver, 1986 Chevy with, of course, the most important feature; a high-power sound system. So Clint took my little Dodge Stratus to Saskatchewan.

It was time for tryouts and exhibition games for the Saskatchewan Junior Hockey League (SJHL). Every player who wanted a spot on the team had to perform well, and regular-season rules were relaxed a bit, especially for hitting and fighting. In the first game, on home ice, Clint got hit from behind. He was reaching for the puck and, as a forward,

Clint's first Truck—a 1986 Chevrolet. In October 1998, it struck a moose, got broken into, and then was stolen out right.

he wore light padding. He took the hit between the top of his pants and the bottom of his upper torso padding. He stroked and glided off the ice, half dragging one leg. He sat out the rest of the first period and the second, but was out in the third. He threw his body around, took some more hits, made a slap shot for a goal and got in a fight. He was hurting quite a bit but wouldn't let on it was bothering him. He didn't want to miss playing any hockey!

Next night it was off to Labret. These are the archrivals, on their ice. The game was intense, and Clint played the best he could, again scoring goals, making plays, taking and giving hits, and getting in a few scuffles. But it caught up to him and, before the game was over, he went to the bench dragging one leg behind him.

He was persuaded to drive to Regina the next day to see a doctor and get X-rays. But he had to battle the health-care professionals to convince them he needed an X-ray (he has those tough Atkinson genes and did not show any distress). They suddenly started fussing over him, however, when the X-ray revealed he had a fracture of his twelfth thoracic vertebra and two ribs.

Didn't I tell you the Atkinsons are tough? After four weeks of healing, he was back on the ice. It usually takes six weeks to heal sufficiently to say you're better; bones usually need another year or two to completely ossify after they've been compromised like that. But Clint was back in competitive, hard-hitting hockey in four weeks. Of course, young, strong athletes tend to heal faster than the rest of us, and we understood that the fracture involved the vertebra's transverse process, which meant that the body of the bone was intact and there was no immediate danger to the spinal chord. But athletes tend to push themselves further and harder than others, too, and Terry and I were still concerned. Pain is a defence mechanism, there to protect you. With Clint's high pain tolerance, it was hard to determine whether he really was ready to be back on the ice. Besides, this is my precious son we're talking about! So we decided to go to see him. We'd take his truck, exchange vehicles, see for ourselves that he was okay, and take in some entertaining hockey while we were at it. The Hounds were to play two games in North Battleford and then a home game right after that. We usually drove through North Battleford before heading south toward Regina and Wilcox anyway, so we decided to take in the games. We started out about seven on a dark and frosty October morning and had been on the road for about an hour when I found the interior light cover lying loose in the cab. I was trying to put it back in its place when it happened. Terry was clipping along at a pretty good pace—not having a properly functioning speedometer, he isn't sure just how fast he was going at the time, probably 110 or 120 kilometres an hour. A moose came out on the road ahead and Terry knew another could be on its heels. Lights from another vehicle were meeting us in the oncoming lane. Terry's amazing reflexes saved our lives.

I remember a swerve, a curse, and a moose filling the entire windshield. I screamed and squeezed the plastic light cover so hard the plastic shattered, sending shrapnel all over the inside of the truck. Terry swerved toward the ditch, catching the hindquarters of a second moose with the driver's side front corner of the truck, sending the poor animal into the air and into the oncoming traffic. The lights heading toward us belonged to a big transport truck. We hit the moose and—vroom!—the truck shot by us. We came to a stop and heard tires squealing down the highway behind us. Terry saw smoke from the burning rubber of the locked-up tires of the transport truck in the rear-view mirror.

Once we knew we were okay, Terry headed down the highway on foot, following a trail of bits of our truck strewn along the lane. He got all the way to the other truck before the shaken driver climbed out. He didn't even hit the step on his way out of the cab; he dropped right from his seat to the pavement. He was glad to know we were okay, but he was shaken up. He had just been driving down a quiet section of unremarkable highway when a moose flew by his windshield; he swerved and it clipped his air cleaner on the way by. He thought he was dead, and I could identify with that feeling. When you see a moose in that much of your window, you can almost guarantee that its next stop is your lap! That's 1,000 pounds or more of injured and scared wild beast hitting us with that horrific impact, flying over the hood and crushing us under its flailing body. Thank goodness for Terry's quick action: we only clipped it, but imagine the force that sent it airborne past the windshield of a semi-trailer rig! We neither saw nor heard the moose after the collision. We regained our composure and assessed the damage. The grill of Clint's truck was broken and bent and, although the headlight was working, the glass was broken, the frame was bent, and the driver's-side rear-view mirror was gone. We decided we could keep going and call our insurance company en route. As we continued down the road, one light illuminated the highway and the other pointed into the ditch, as if scanning for more moose! When we passed a vehicle going the same direction as we, it looked as though we had a spotlight shining in on them as we drove by. But our truck was driveable and, although shaken, we were okay. We arrived in North Battleford and found the hockey team. We stayed at the same hotel as the boys and got a chance to visit Clint. He was glad to see us and his beloved truck, even though we'd "grilled Moose" on it the day before. Clint looked strong and healthy and played a good game that night. The next day, a Sunday, we packed up and checked out of the hotel before heading over to the arena. We put all our bags in the cab of the truck so we could lock them in for safe-keeping. After the game, we waited to say farewell to Clint as he loaded up on the bus to head back to Wilcox. When we walked back to our truck, a frightening sight met our eyes: The truck had been broken into. Damage to a window and door showed where the thieves gained entry. Some of our bags had been ransacked, the stereo system had been removed, the CDs, and the sub-woofer speakers behind the seats were gone. Terry had left his wallet in the glove box and that was gone, too. However, he had left cash in one of my bags and the thieves hadn't touched it. We couldn't believe it, this run of bad luck! We were upset (Terry used a few colourful phrases), and we started calling banks, credit-card companies, our insurance company (again) and the RCMP. Another huge hassle, but we continued on our way.

Driving through Saskatoon, a tree was lying across our off-ramp, and Terry's reflexes saved us from yet another disaster as he swerved around it, driving over the upper limbs instead of the trunk. After removing my fingers from the dashboard, where they'd been embedded, and catching my breath, I laughed in disbelief: "There's one tree in Saskatoon and it's lying across our off-ramp!" Of course, I was exaggerating. Saskatchewan, particularly the northern part of the province, is filled with beautiful forests and lakes. It's southern Saskatchewan that most people are thinking of in their image of the province as flat and treeless. It was just that I was amazed at our luck thus far during the trip. Well, maybe that was number three and we wouldn't have any more surprises. Wrong!

We finally got settled in a hotel in Regina and had a bite to eat and a bit of rest before driving the half-hour south to Wilcox to watch more hockey. The drive to Wilcox allows one to experience the stereotypical landscape of the province of "the land of the living skies". It seems as if you can see Wilcox 15 minutes before you even reach the turn off the highway. I remember Clint's first winter there. He called home and told us, "It snows sideways out here!" The only trees are those that have been planted in yards; otherwise, nothing breaks the horizon. They tease that you can see your dog run away from home for three days.

We arrived at the beautiful arena in the tiny hamlet of Wilcox just as the Hounds were warming up on the Olympic-sized ice surface. We paid our admission and I casually mentioned to Terry, "I'm going to the can." Terry said he was heading right out to the bleachers to watch warm ups.

As you first step into this building, there are doors ahead of you and doors to the right. The doors to the right lead into another part of the building that houses classrooms, the library, gymnasium, and more. The doors ahead are open to a small set of stairs leading up to a huge hall or mezzanine. Stairs to the left lead down to the trainer's room, dressing rooms, laundry, and skate-sharpening room. As you reach the top of the stairs, the mezzanine sprawls in front of you with picnic tables, counters and garbage receptacles running down the centre of it.

Along the wall to your right is a Wall of Scholarships and a Wall of Fame, a wall of history and achievement containing many faces you might recognize: pictures of people like Father David William Bauer, the Basilian priest and hockey coach; Canada's 1964 Olympic team; and hockey stars such as Curtis Joseph, Wendell Clarke, Rod Brind'Amour, Gary Leeman and the like—an entire wall of Notre Dame athletes who went into professional sports or obtained athletic scholarships to prestigious colleges and universities all over the world, not just in hockey, but in football, baseball, and other sports. The hall also offers play stations (video games), a banking machine and a TV. In the corner, a glass cabinet displays memorabilia, awards, and trophies.

One side of the mezzanine is a wall of glass overlooking the ice surface.

Hockey arena at the Althol Murray College of Notre Dame in Wilcox, Saskatchewan, Canada.

Looking out that window you can see the ice from end to end. At the end of the rink, the electronic time clock and scoreboard tops a huge red-and-white banner showing a Hound symbol framing the words "Never Loose Heart". From the roof hangs banner after banner showing the championships won by Hounds. Everywhere—on walls, in corners and spread across ceilings—there are plaques, pictures, emblems, awards, jerseys framed and signed, and framed newspaper and magazine articles praising the athletic and academic prowess of Notre Dame.

You'll also see the Notre Dame Crest in various places throughout the complex proclaiming, "Luctor et Emergo" ["I Struggle and Emerge"].

This is a "feel-good place" and one where I feel quite at home. This is where we were—home ice, getting ready for another exciting game of Junior Hockey. But when I returned from my visit to the restroom, Terry was not on our usual bench. I assumed he must have decided to get a coffee. Maybe I walked past him on my way out to the rink and didn't see him at the concession. I was hoping he'd bring me a hot chocolate. The boys had finished their pre-game warm ups, and still no Terry. I still wasn't concerned; he probably found some one to chat with. Then a lady approached me and said, "Excuse me. That gentleman you came in with. He got hit in the head with the puck; I think he's in the trainer's room."

"No way!" I laughed out loud. This was just too much. I followed a trail of blood drops to the room where Tom, the team trainer, was doing his best for Terry. My poor husband was as angry as a hornet, lying on a table arguing with the rotund and very knowledgeable Tom.

"Just stitch me up!" Terry was saying.

"I can't," Tom said; "it's not within my scope of practice. You need to go to the hospital"

"No damn way!" Terry retorted. "I came to watch hockey, and that's what I'm going to do. Give me a needle and thread and I'll do it myself! Either sew me up or I'll do it."

"Okay, okay," Tom conceded, "I can put steristrips on, but you really should have stitches and have a doctor look at you. I can't promise you these closures will do the job."

An impatient Terry interrupted him, "Just do it!"

I listened to this as I watched blood leaking from above Terry's right eye while he dabbed at it with a bloody dressing. Terry had just opened the doors and stepped into the rink when the coaches up on the bleachers to his left hollered, "Hi Terry!" As he glanced up, a puck with the momentum of a slap shot hit the cross bar off the net and went airborne, flying over the glass and hitting Terry's forehead just above his eye.

It sent his glasses into the bleachers in two pieces. Blood immediately started gushing from the slice above his eye, and he went temporarily blind from the impact and the blood running into his eye. He had his eyes closed as he put pressure on the gash with one hand and tried to gain his balance and composure. He was leaning forward, trying to keep from bleeding all over his shirt and leather jacket, when someone grabbed him from behind, trying to lead him to Tom for first aid. It was the iceman, the rink attendant, the arena maintenance guy—whatever you want to call him. I'm sure any name you come up with would be a lot more suitable to print than the flurry of names and suggestions that spewed from Terry's lips! Injured, bleeding, and temporarily blind, with blood stinging his eyes and bells ringing in his head, the last thing Terry wanted was to be wrestled by a well-meaning Good Samaritan. When Terry's hurt, he gets mad and mean. He also requires a very large personal space. The poor rink attendant had great intentions, but they certainly weren't well received. I believe Terry sent him on his way after they negotiated the stairs and Terry's sharp tongue gave him some colourful directions.

Terry never did see a doctor and healed quite nicely. Tom did an exceptional job with those skin closures. You can't even see any scarring! Terry's glasses needed only minor repair. The lens flew out, but didn't break, and the frame, although bent, worked well enough to hold the lens in place and balance across Terry's face, allowing him to see the game and cheer the boys on. When I think about all these things, I don't know whether they are spells of bad luck or good luck. People have died hitting moose and trees, getting robbed, and being struck on the head. Nonetheless, I figured, the tree wasn't that bad; maybe it wasn't the third bad-luck event. But this one has to be it; now we're done.

Not quite.

We had spent a lot of our time in Saskatchewan running the truck here and there for estimates on repairs, filing reports with the RCMP, and talking to Insurance representatives. We bought Clint a brand new pair of skates and said goodbye. We headed home, driving my little red car, and left Clint his "baby," battered as it was. We had a thankfully uneventful trip home but hadn't been back four days when Clint called. His girlfriend from Grande Prairie had been down to visit him and they had gone into Regina for the day. They went to a movie and, when they came out, his truck was gone. He had his new skates behind the seat, as he had brought them in to have the blades balanced and aligned. He had parked under a streetlight and locked up. We never saw that truck again. More police reports, more lists of what was missing, more calls to insurance companies. That was our October.

"What next?" I shouldn't have asked that. The question seems to imply that you are expecting more to come, almost inviting another unfortunate event. Never say, "What's next?" I sure wish I hadn't. It was now November 10, 1998, and our daughters would be getting a day off school the next day for Remembrance Day. Jessie and Erin took my car into town to hang out with some friends. They said they might go to a party later and would call. At about 10:30 pm, they phoned to say that they were at a party in the country out by Clairmont, a small bedroom community north of Grande Prairie. They had been to the house before, the parents were home, and could they please stay longer. I asked them to come home. "The weather's bad," I told them; "there's a blizzard bearing down, the roads are icy, it's dark, you're a young driver, and it's a long weekend. All the cards are stacked against you. Dad and I would feel better if you started home right away."

Jessie didn't even put up an argument. She just said okay. Sometimes they wanted to be told to come home. If they didn't really want to be somewhere, it was a good excuse to leave when Mom and Dad told them they had to. This might have been the case, or perhaps she heard the worry in my voice, or it could have been that what I said made sense to her, too. In any case, I remember being surprised that I didn't get any guff and they said they were on their way. By midnight, however, they still hadn't reached our acreage home just west of Grande Prairie. It should take about three quarters of an hour on good roads, maybe an hour or so on bad ones, but it was now over two hours. Terry and I were in bed, but we weren't sleeping soundly. Our ears were tuned for the distinctive sounds of tires creeping along on the gravel and the purring of a motor slowly coming to a stop in our driveway. Instead, we jumped alert when the telephone rang. Jessie's voice was shaking, sobbing, and upset. I could barely understand what she was trying to say.

"Mom," came through the sobs.

"Where are you?" I asked, Anxiety was starting to put a stranglehold on my chest.

"At the hospital; we had an accident," Jessie sobbed.

I could barely get the words out of my mouth as I felt my throat starting to tighten. "Are you okay?" I croaked.

"Well," she began, "Trisha and I are."

There was a second of silence as I computed the words I just heard.

"And Erin?" I heard the panic in my voice. I felt as though I was choking on my heart.

"She can't feel her legs" I heard through the thumping in my brain.

I don't recall what I said. I just remember flying out of bed and grabbing clothes to put on as I stumbled in the dark and in a daze. I was shaking and could barely breathe. Terry was mad. He was scared, too, but he showed only his anger.

Anger is the only emotion Terry let anyone see, although he felt the whole range of emotions, as I did. He bellowed at me the whole way to the hospital. I cried. We were both really scared and feeling helpless. He showed it his way and I mine. Jessie was visibly shaken and panic-stricken but surrounded by friends offering her support and comfort. There were a lot of kids, it seemed, hovering, pacing, and sitting with faces showing fear and disbelief. After hugging Jessie, we went right into the trauma room to see our baby strapped to a spine board, in agony. She could feel her legs. She was complaining about the pain in her back. They had just taken X-rays, and we were about to hear the results. A doctor, looking as if he just graduated from high school, told us that Erin had a stable fracture of the second lumbar vertebra. The spinose process had been broken. The body of the vertebra was okay—therefore her spinal chord still had adequate protection—but one of the little pieces of bone that you can feel when you hunch your back and run your fingers along the spine had been broken off. They were going to give her some morphine and stand her up. We could take her home. Remember my telling you how tough the Atkinsons are and what high pain tolerance they seem to have? Well, Erin is a true Atkinson. I'm the only wimp in the family, I think; I don't take pain very well at all. After the shot of morphine had time to start its "magic" and the staff "perched" her on the edge of the table in preparation for standing her up, sweat broke out in beads across her nose and she yelled. I knew she was hurt badly. I stood in front of her, supporting her. As she tried to stand, she literally passed out in my arms. "Help me lay her back down!" I hollered. I heard the doctor call for a wheelchair. I couldn't believe my ears. I'm holding an unconscious child in my arms and they want me to put her in a wheelchair! They refused to lay her back down and helped me seat her in the chair wheeled into the room. She kept going in and out of consciousness. They would argue that she was just responding to the morphine. But I could see by her pale face, her breathing pattern, and the sweat that she was in pain, and that was at least part of the reason for her periods of unresponsiveness.

Meanwhile, Terry was restless and had already spoken to the kids and the cop, piecing the story together. He had lectured each of the kids and was fighting with the staff in the hallway while the doctor was insisting we take Erin home. I could hear Terry, voice raised, saying things like, "How do you propose we do that?" and "How do we get her in our vehicle?"

I heard the doctor calmly ask, "What kind of car do you have?"

"It's a truck," Terry responded, "And it makes no difference because she's staying here."

"And on what grounds do you think I should admit her?" asked Doogie Howser.

Terry almost came completely unglued. I could tell it was taking all the energy he could muster not to tear that poor guy limb from limb.

"I don't care," he raged, "just do it!"

This was the gist of the argument between them. Finally the doc came back into the trauma room to encourage Erin to buck up and try to move on her own. Terry was pacing like a caged wild animal in the hallway, barely holding on to his restraint.

I told the doctor: "Look, you don't understand. She needs to stay here at least for overnight and you need to find her a bed. Are you listening to me? Either you get her a bed or you are going to need one because I cannot be responsible for what her dad will do to you if you don't."

She was admitted. She stayed there five days. She had difficulty moving, walking, and sitting, and she couldn't void her bowels. She had blood in her urine. They put a lift on her toilet seat, something I had asked for. No one seemed to know what I was talking about until a wonderful nurse, who worked a lot on the orthopaedic floor and was doing a few shifts on paediatrics, went and got one. They also got her a walker to help her get around. They taught her how to get in and out of bed properly. She couldn't sit, just "perch," stand, or lie down. An ultrasound showed swelling and bruising to some of her internal organs. They gave her stool softeners, but they weren't doing the job, so I would tell the nurses I would make sure she got her pills, then toss them into the garbage and give her herbs. That helped her a lot.

We put magnets on her back and she started feeling better. But we couldn't seem to find anything that would help her manage her pain adequately. As time went on, she became "used" to the pain at a certain level of intensity. She only complained if it peaked. I must tell you that the level of pain she became accustomed to would have been agony for a lot of people—me, for one. One thing that shocked Erin was all the people who came to visit her in the hospital—her friends, Jessie's friends, Clint's friends, family, and acquaintances she met at the party that night. She was overwhelmed at how many people cared about her and wanted to wish her well. .

"I can't believe I have all these friends", she told me. "Why do all these people come to see me? I don't even know some of them very well and they're all so concerned about *me*!" She was truly sincere in her disbelief and wonder, and she was very grateful.

I asked her about the crash. I try not to use the term "accident". An accident implies that an event was unavoidable. Usually what we call "accidents" are both predictable and preventable. This one was. Between Erin and Jessie, the story went something like this: Shortly after calling home and speaking with me, the girls left the party. Trisha Stienke, Erin's friend, sat in the front passenger seat. Jessie drove. Erin sat in the middle of the back seat. All put their seatbelts on. Of course they were dressed for a social gathering, not the weather. Vehicles had pulled into the driveway behind them and they could not leave the same way they had arrived. Having been there before, however, Jessie knew of another route. A private road led to the house from another side, so they drove around the house and left that way. That road connected with a range road. Jessie knew it was a bit of a drive and that the road she was on would end at a T intersection. It was pitch black and the snow was coming down hard, so it was very hard to see, and she found herself using the fence line that ran parallel to the road as a marker. The problem was that the fence line jumped the range road, and kept going on the other side where there was no more road.

Just as the driveway comes to an end, it reaches a small rise or incline. Watching the fence line stretch on ahead of her, Jessie never even slowed down. She didn't see the range road until she went over the rise and was on it. She reacted as fast as she could, and she remembered from driver's training that she shouldn't swerve or she would end up on her roof. She took the ditch head-on and they braced for impact. That ditch, unfortunately, was back cut, so the facing bank was quite steep, and the collision was like hitting a wall. The RCMP officer who investigated told us he almost piled in behind her. He could understand how easy it was to miss that intersection. Nevertheless, the girls had been travelling too fast for the conditions—the officer estimated between 60 and 80 kilometres an hour. The impact activated the air bags. The girls in front were bruised and shaken, and Trisha had a small cut on her face, probably from the air bag cover. There was a cloud of white dust in the air and a "funny smell." Thanks to Hollywood—and the chemical smell from the air bags—the girls thought the car was about to explode. It makes sense. First the crash, then "kaboom!" That's what happens in the movies all the time, and they had seen "smoke." They started screaming at each other to "get out, *get out!*" Jessie and Trisha were out like bullets. Erin was struggling. She finally released the lap belt and rolled out of the car into the snowy ditch where she was stuck on her hands and knees. "I can't move," she cried. Jessie and Trisha began to panic.

"Look", Erin told them, "one of you has to stay with me and one has to run back to the house for help." Jessie would go. She left on a dead run. Erin said that Trisha was very upset. If you know her story, you'd understand. Sometimes when I think about how many hard knocks we have had to take and start feeling sorry for myself, I think about what Trisha's family has had to go through—a truly traumatic story. Then I feel ashamed. No wonder poor Trisha was upset. Erin tried to console her. She was also worried about Jessie. Jessie suffered from exercise-induced asthma, which is aggravated by cold, dry air. Erin was afraid Jessie would have an attack while running in this weather.

"Mom," she said, "I prayed that Jessie would be okay." Jessie told me later that she did have difficulty breathing and at one point collapsed on the road, out of air and exhausted. When she told herself her sister needed her, she found the strength within her to carry on. Do you see the power of love, the power of prayer?

As Erin was telling this story I stopped her at this point. "Let me get this straight," I said. "You were in so much pain that you couldn't move. You were not dressed for the weather and were on your hands and knees in the snowy, dark ditch in the middle of a blizzard. And it is you who console a friend and are so concerned about your sister's health that you pray she'll be okay. Have I got that right?"

She looked at me with a question in her eyes, as she didn't know where I was going with this.

"Honey," I continued, "how can you tell me that you have no idea why you have so many people expressing their love and concern for you? It's because of who you are—that wonderful, selfless, genuine, and sincere spirit that is you, who shows that strength of character when the chips are down. You just told me why they all love you, sweetheart: Because you are you, you are special, and friends like you are a rare and precious gift. These people who have come by or sent greetings are smart enough to know that they are blessed to know you."

After a brief intermission of hugs, kisses and I-love-yous all around, I urged the girls to continue their story. Jessie had stumbled and fallen a few times on her way for help with the thought of her sister pushing her on. She got to the house and told the story. Kids piled into vehicles and raced to the scene. They loaded the girls into cars and trucks and headed for the hospital. No one thought to wake the parents and let them know. No one had called 911. Erin was transported in a truck with her head lying on the driver's lap and her body on the bench seat. I can imagine the panic and driving tactics of a young man in his truck on gravel roads in winter, but they all got to the hospital safely. It was the hospital staff that immobilized Erin on the backboard.

Both Terry and I spoke to the kids at the hospital. We thanked them, but we lectured, too. Maybe adults could have been informed; maybe someone should have called for an ambulance. They had a pretty good rebuttal, though. They had been concerned about the cold and felt they needed to get them all into warm, dry vehicles. Good call. How do you argue with that logic? Once there, they thought it would be saving time to take them to the hospital themselves.

When all is said and done and you look back on this event years later, those kids did the best they could and made some hard decisions. They acted quickly and stuck around after getting to the hospital, providing moral support for Jessie and for one another. Good kids. Thank you again, guys, for being there.

After Erin got home from the hospital, it was a week before she could get dressed, get in and out of bed, and use the walker without help. Another week and she was back at high school. Icy walks, crowded halls, kids roughhousing, carrying books, and sitting for eighty-minute classes seemed too much for a healing back. By the next report card, we understood how she coped—she skipped classes a lot. She was so far behind in school that when she went back after the crash it was easier to skip than to try to catch up. Before Christmas, I phoned our family doctor. I told him I wanted Erin to have another X-ray to see how she was healing. She was still in a lot of pain, and before she started any physiotherapy, I wanted to make sure she was healing okay. I had to explain and insist. He didn't think another X-ray was warranted.

In fact, he thought it would be an unnecessary further exposure to radiation and a waste of resources. But I was determined, and she went for her X-ray. That same day we received a phone call from our doctor's nurse.

"We have Erin booked for a follow-up CT scan" she informed us. I asked her why. What had they seen? She told me she wasn't qualified to discuss it but I pushed her: *"What did you see?"* She finally responded nervously that a slight irregularity showed up that they wanted to have a better look at. We went for the scan.

Remember, Erin was doing as much as she was able. She had been told that the only thing stopping her from her regular activities was her pain. So she had been pushing herself and tried to get back into life again, doing as much as she could, doing stretches and exercises to strengthen her back. But the pain and deformity—she called herself 'Erin the two-humped camel'—were constant companions. She walked into diagnostic imaging. After the CT scan, the radiologist walked past me in the hall a few times, then said, "We're running another scan. We just want to be sure. We found some—well there seems to be—well, come and see."

He led me into the viewing room. CT films were lined up against the light panels. He pointed out her vertebra, but even my untrained eye could see it. I uttered an expletive as I stared in disbelief at Erin's second lumbar vertebra. The body of the bone was riddled with fracture lines. I was ill. The radiologist suggested that she see an orthopaedic specialist in outpatients before we go, but she already had an appointment. He was relieved to hear it.

They told Erin only that she needed to stay on the stretcher as they wheeled her to the outpatient department. We waited. She needed to pee. No one would let her off the stretcher.

"What's going on?" she demanded. "I walk in here and now they won't let me up. Something isn't right; what did they find?" I told her.

The specialist finally arrived and, after a look at the pictures and a little chat with Erin, ordered a Clamshell cast. My background told me that this might not be the appropriate treatment at this time. A cast like that would have been ordered as soon as the injury occurred, but not now. He gasped when I reminded him that she had suffered the injury about three weeks earlier. That changed everything. He cancelled the cast and ordered a Jewett brace. When she got up to pee, I asked about the deformity. That, I was told, would be like the chronic pain: she'd have to live with both. She was fitted for the brace before we left the hospital and I phoned Terry. You can probably imagine what he thought about the whole thing.

Erin was told she would have to wear the brace for four to six weeks and could take it off only for bathing. After that she could use it as necessary for added support if she wanted. I found out later that she wore the thing all the time only for about a week and took it off at bedtime so she could get a comfortable night's sleep. Then she started removing it at school, as it would squeak when she breathed and she was teased. After the brace was no longer required, she was encouraged to lead a normal life. Again she was told she would always have pain and the lumps on her back. She was only 15.

Back at school through all this, she kept up with those negative habits that she had picked up the semester before—show up for some classes but skip most. She failed Grade 10.

"What are we going to do with you?" we asked—the usual parental rhetorical question. "Maybe we should send you to Notre Dame!"

This was meant to scare her. Notre Dame is for the bright academic achiever, the athlete, and of course the problem student— a last chance for parents hoping that this private school can straighten out their wayward child. A lot of kids don't like the discipline and structure. They don't like being away from home and being totally responsible for their actions, and they don't like the isolation of a little a town on the vast expanse of Saskatchewan prairie. But Erin surprised us with her response.

"Could I go?" she asked eagerly. "Really?"

She had never mentioned it before, but ever since visiting Clint there, she had secretly fantasized about being one of those kids—a Notre Dame Hound (student). We were caught a bit off guard and said we'd think about it.

It was summertime. A spunky little soul, Erin wouldn't let a little thing like pain stop her, and now she had another reason to try harder to show she was okay. She wanted to go to school away from home. That summer, while we were seriously considering sending Erin to Notre Dame, we went water sliding, hiking, canoeing, and white-water rafting. Every night, Erin would sob in pain—but as discreetly as she could. When asked if she was okay, she would say yes. We tried to ease her pain with heat or cold, stretches or massage, whatever we could do. We'd always ask, "Are you sure you feel up to this?" before we did any of the activities. All she could think of was how she wasn't going to let her back pain stop her from living and doing the things she loved. Every morning she struggled out of bed, stiff and sometimes sore enough to draw some tears, but never enough to keep her from having fun, and certainly not enough to complain about. Summer was drawing to a close. We decided that since Clint's marks, attitude, and maturity had flourished at ND, perhaps that was the best place for Erin, too. After all, she'd have it easier than her brother.

Although not a student any more, Clint would still be living in Wilcox and playing junior hockey there, so she'd have family close by. We started getting all the paperwork done and sent for Erin's registration to Notre Dame. One of the items required is a doctor's report, a physical, and any information on health pertinent to the health-care department at the school. Erin's doctor gave a history of her back and a clean bill of health. Again, the only thing preventing her from doing anything was her pain. Pain is a body's defence mechanism, as I've said before. If it hurts, stop, but don't ignore it. The pain is telling you that you may be damaging your body. Listen to that warning. But that wasn't the message Erin was getting. She heard that if she couldn't do everything she tried to do, she was a wimp. Our concern was that she was still in so much pain. She really wanted to try out for the volleyball team. Terry wasn't satisfied—she would be so far away from us. There was no way our little girl should have to suffer pain the rest of her life. He wanted another doctor's opinion, and he wanted one from someone other than a doctor in Grande Prairie. As Insurance companies were involved (because of the way her injuries occurred), Terry approached them to get her checked out by one of their physicians. After some insistence, that, too, was arranged. Jessie, Erin, and I went to Edmonton to see the doctor. We got to the office early and Erin tried the door. It was still locked. We were waiting in the car by the curb when an elderly gentleman approached the door. Erin got out and said, "It's still locked!"

"Yes", replied the man, "I know; I have the key!" We were impressed right away with his friendly, grandfatherly style. He invited us all inside and excused himself to get set up and organized before he called us into his office. Again I was impressed as I watched and listened. Not one doctor we had seen thus far had actually taken the time to sit and listen to Erin, looking at her as she spoke before he made his notes. He was listening with courtesy and caring. We didn't feel we had to hurry and get out of his hair because he needed to be somewhere else. And the exam! That was more thorough than others she had gone through, but certainly not so complex that any one of the other physicians couldn't have done it. It intrigued me when he placed two fingers between the lumps in her back and had her flex and then straighten up, over and over. Finally he explained that he was trying to feel for any gap in the deformity when she flexed her back. He shook his head. He was having too much trouble trying to determine a gap by palpation. He said he would like an X-ray, if that was all right. Of course, we said yes. He picked up the phone and called the imaging lab himself.

He told the receptionist that he wanted to speak to the technician taking the pictures. "No," he said with a sternness and impatience in his voice that was new to us, "I said the actual technician, do you understand? The guy taking the pictures. Let me speak to him directly. Look, just get him."

He told us while he was on hold to go to the building at the corner of the street and up to the floor for diagnostic imaging. He wanted us to wait until the pictures were done and bring them back to him right away. We did.

The reason he wanted to speak to the tech was to ensure that they understood exactly what he wanted: pictures of Erin's back in the flexion position, something no one had done. As soon as we returned, we handed the folder to a receptionist now at a desk in the front office. The doctor was with another patient but had obviously left directions that he wanted to see us as soon as we got back with the X-rays because the receptionist went right into the room where he was, and when she came out he was right behind her, carrying the folder. He motioned us into the next room and pulled the film out of the folder, sliding it snugly into place on the backlit panel. After only a second he said, "Well, this is exactly what I didn't want to see." He explained that Erin had a "chance" fracture caused by a violent pulling apart of the structures in her back. Often the action causes damage to soft tissue only, but in this case the bone itself had actually been pulled apart.

The X-ray clearly showed Erin's spine in a slight bend forward (flexion position) and, even with that slight forward bend, you could see a large enough gap to expose her spinal chord; there was no bone structure protecting it. I was almost sick to my stomach in that instant of realization. I thought of all the activities of the summer. I could see her in my memories as though watching an old 1950s-style home movie flickering through my brain. I saw her bumping and slipping along on the water slides and trying to qualify for white-water rafting. She had to be able to paddle the loaded, six-person raft around 360 degrees by herself against a current. I saw her dad helping her with stretches at night that had her bending, and the jumping and twisting she did while playing volleyball against her sister. As I write this I feel the nausea and anxiety rising up within me all over again. My God.

"What do you suggest should be the next move?" I heard myself say. He gave us options. Surgery was one, but he said that if she were his child, he'd have the surgery done right away. I understood. If we got rear-ended, even slightly, at an intersection while leaving the city, Jessie and I might get a mild whiplash, but Erin could be paralysed. Heavens, she could trip over a curb and end up in a wheelchair for life! It was only by the grace of God that she was still okay; I knew it. This doctor, whom we had all come to trust in such a short while, made some phone calls. "Can you be at the Royal Alexandra Hospital tomorrow morning to see a surgeon?" he asked us. "I'd like him to take a look, and then you'd have his opinion, too."

We left that doctor's office after expressing our gratitude for his help, although that didn't seem enough. We never saw that physician again, but he was an angel. We were sent to Erin's own guardian angel and we will never be able to thank him enough for his compassion and wisdom. Why aren't there more doctors like him? Terry and I spoke at length on the phone that evening and decided that I would fill him in again after Erin's visit with the surgeon, but I wouldn't make any decision regarding surgery until we could all talk about it together. We found out later that while I was talking to Terry that evening from our hotel room, that sweet, grandfatherly doctor was at home discussing Erin on the phone with another surgeon at *his* home. I hadn't seen this kind of care in a long while. It was as though Erin mattered to them as much as she does to us. At the Royal Alexandra Hospital outpatient department, we saw the surgeon who had been filled in about Erin on the phone the night before. It was as if everyone knew us; we were a priority. The surgeon explained the procedure he suggested. "If I could," he said, "I would perform this surgery immediately. However, because this injury occurred so long ago, I wouldn't be able to justify it as an emergency."

He felt that he might be able to get her in early next week but couldn't promise anything and suggested we go home. They would call us when a time was available. Both doctors said very similar things, and I could sense the urgency both in the way they came across to us and in the urgency of our appointment with the surgeon. Terry and I decided to go with this procedure. Erin needed a "spinal fusion with instrumentation" to strengthen her back and protect her spinal chord.

Friday morning we headed home and arrived in late afternoon to discover a voice-mail message from the hospital asking us to bring Erin in for magnetic resonance imaging (MRI) that afternoon. Obviously, they didn't understand that we lived a good five-hour drive away. We called back and rescheduled. Arrangements were made for an MRI on Monday, admission to hospital Tuesday afternoon, and surgery Wednesday morning, September 1, 1999. That was the same day we had planned to leave for Saskatchewan to register Erin at Notre Dame.

It was a different surgeon who visited Erin on admission on Tuesday. We had expected that, as the first surgeon had said he wouldn't be available. But Dr. Mahood also impressed us with his sincerity. He never once stood by the door as if he was waiting to dart out any second; he never looked anxiously at his watch. He seemed to have all the time in the world for us and gave us his undivided attention. An air of confidence and compassion wafted from him like a tangible essence, and even though we were all nervous, we trusted him.

Terry had come to Edmonton with us this time. He wouldn't dream of letting Erin go through this without us being there for her. Clint had already been at Notre Dame for about a week for hockey camp, but he was with us in spirit. We tried to keep him informed when we could. He hadn't been billeted yet, so he was relying on pay phones, and of course we couldn't have Terry's cell phone on in the hospital, so communication was difficult. Clint expected this, so we scheduled times when he could call. We were all concerned, but Jessie was especially upset. Erin was more than her sister; she was a soul mate and best friend, part of her entire being. Jessie felt completely responsible for all that had happened to Erin and all the suffering she had endured. She called Erin her little Winkie Doodlebug, and the two were as inseparable as two peas in a pod—when you saw one, you knew the other wasn't far away. Even though each had her own bedroom at home, whenever we went to wake them in the morning, Jessie would be in Erin's bed with her, or visa versa. They even invented their own language. People thought they were twins—not because they looked alike (they were very different in appearance)—but because of how they interacted with each other. They were like two separate parts of the same person. Jessie felt as if she had wounded a part of herself and was feeling the pain intensely. On Wednesday we gave Erin hugs and kisses, told her how much we loved her, and watched her roll down the hallway to surgery. I stayed by her side until she was actually wheeled into the operating room. It was six hours before we saw her again. Lines and tubes were running in and out of her. She looked like a helpless cyborg connected to machines, bags and poles. Her face was terribly swollen from being face down on the operating table for four hours. It had been framed by a donut-shaped table end supporting her head. The procedure usually takes about two hours, we were told, but scar tissue had to be removed first and that extended the surgery. Two rods were placed alongside her backbone to provide support. They were held in place by three embedded screws, and one hook that attached to the vertebra. Two horizontal clasps or bars were placed between the rods. All this metal was necessary to keep the bones from moving while the spine fused. This would be accomplished by laying pieces of bone taken from Erin's ileac crest (hip bone) along the fractured vertebra (L2) and the stable vertebra next to it (L3). Over time, the new bone chips they added would grow and encase the two vertebrae with solid bone, a fusion. Remember, a broken bone is usually stable and strong after six weeks of healing, but takes two years to ossify into really strong, solid bone. Poor Winkie. She was sore and groggy. She was hooked to a PCA (patient controlled analgesic) machine, which allowed her to push a button to deliver a dose of intravenous morphine. The machine is set so that a precise dose is delivered, and it is programmed to deliver it only if enough time has passed since the last dose. The machine records how many doses are delivered and when and how many times the patient pushed the button. This helps staff to determine whether the patient is getting adequate pain control.

Unfortunately, narcotics like morphine tend to have nasty side effects. As time wore on, Erin began to suffer from these: she still hurt, but she was also nauseated, itchy and bitchy, and occasionally anything but lucid. Jessie didn't want to leave her sister's side. We all acted as advocates, ensuring that Erin had everything she needed. It was hard on all of us, not just poor little Winkie Doodlebug! They started her on

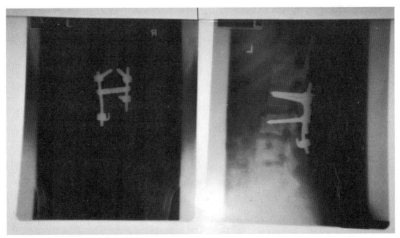

These are photos of the x-rays of Erin's back after her surgery in 1999. The left picture is like standing behind Erin who has her back to you. The right photo is looking at her from her left side.

intravenous Benadryl to help control the itching, and added Gravol for nausea the drugs were causing, but she was still hurting. Nothing seemed to be doing what it was supposed to. We had her narcotic changed to Demerol, but still she was miserable. I think Terry, as a father, was having trouble seeing his baby in such pain when he had no control over the situation. He wanted to protect her and save her from all this misery. He spent a lot of time discussing alternatives with the doctor and staff. He wanted to know every drug that was going into her, why she was on it, and what it was doing to her. He sat and read to learn everything he could about each drug. As "Momma," I was doing everything I could to make her comfortable. As a nurse, I was familiar with the environment, the treatment, and the drugs. It hurt me as a mother to see her hurting, but I was confident the pain would eventually subside and she would be better. There was hope; I held on to that. Jessie was guilt-ridden and, as I watched her with her sister, I could see Jessie's love, admiration and a level of patience that I rarely saw. I could see she was inspired by Erin's courage and saddened by feeling responsible for it all.

Erin never blamed Jessie. She never even implied it in the smallest measure. None of us did. But Jessie blamed herself. She was always her own nemesis. The time in hospital wasn't always sad; we also had moments of joy and laughter. One source of the giggles was Erin herself. She was so high on narcotics that she wasn't always occupying the same time and space as the rest of us. I recall Erin's first night after surgery as a rough one. I slept, or had plans to sleep, at the foot of Erin's bed on a small cot the staff supplied for me. I would just get settled and have relaxed my head into the pillow when Erin would call out in a panic to me, "Mom! Mom!" I would spring bolt upright, scrambling to get my feet steady under me. I would be at her bedside in a flash, before my eyes had opened fully. "What? What's wrong?" She would tell me her back was itchy and could I scratch it. Higher, lower, more to the right, more to the left, nothing was working. It was as if the itching was just under the skin and the scratching wasn't reaching it. Could I scratch her legs, too? She couldn't reach them. She would be barking orders with a frustration in her tone that clawed at the air in desperation. She seemed to be jumping and trying to climb out of her skin, all without moving anything but her head, toes, and hands. Just as suddenly as the ranting had begun, it stopped. She was fast asleep, as if someone had flicked an off switch somewhere in her head. I would watch for a second or two to make sure, and then quietly, stealthily, I would slip back into my cramped little cot. I would arrange my pillow, my sheet, my blanket and myself. I'd nestle in and close my eyes. A couple of deep sighs to help me relax, and I could feel the tension in my muscles start to let go. There, now I'll be able to sleep.

"Mom! Mom!" would come the cry, and the whole thing would start again.

During one of these episodes, just as Erin started to drift into sleep, she said ever so sweetly: "Oh Momma, you don't have to stand here all night by my bed. You should go lie down and get some sleep." I smiled. She did this a few times more through the night, and soon I was chuckling to myself. Those very few minutes when she slept felt like hours to her. Every time she closed her eyes, she thought a lot of time had passed. Itchy, Bitchy and Nod—I was trapped in some kind of twisted nursery rhyme, a scene from *The Twilight Zone* with the many faces of Erin. A few days later, Erin had her 16th birthday. The nurses brought in rubber gloves blown up like balloons, with birthday greetings written all over them. They tied them to the bedposts and "monkey bars" hanging over her bed. We had cards and flowers, gifts, trinkets and pictures placed, taped, set, strung and pinned all over her little corner of the world. What a way for a girl to spend her sweet sixteen! Eventually, one by one, tubes and lines, bags and poles were removed from in, on and around our little girl. She started to become more mobile, assisted by a variety of professionals. Pain was one thing; the drugs were another. Every time she was asked about pain, she rated it about a 7 or 8 on the scale from 1 to 10, ten being the worst pain. The staff were attempting to lower those numbers by using drugs. Finally her patience ran out.

"Look," she exclaimed in frustration, "I've lived with my back pain at 8 for a year now, I think I can handle it—just get me off these f—— drugs!" That was our little princess. At least she got her point across. Sometimes it takes strong language to get people's attention and help them understand that you have had enough. They changed her order to oral analgesic, which she would refuse when asked if she needed any. Now that her mind was clearer, she had no more nausea, and she wasn't trying to claw her skin off. When she was finally released, I picked up her prescription for Tylenol 3 (containing codeine). She kept telling me I was wasting my money; she wasn't going to take any, but I knew we had a long drive home. I thought she might need some, at least for the trip. We stopped occasionally on the drive to allow everyone to stretch and walk. Erin never took one of those pills during the six-hour trip. We did eventually send her to Notre Dame in October to take her Grade 10 again. She had missed too much of the first semester to catch up at the Composite High School here in Grande Prairie, but Notre Dame doesn't use the semester system. They said they could catch her up, and they did. Her back continued to cause her anguish, however, and in March 2001 she eventually had the metal removed. Since then, although her back gets tired and aches occasionally, we rarely hear her complain.

CHAPTER SEVEN
Jessie Jean

The extent of our run of luck goes much deeper. We had several fender-benders, rollovers, and serious scares involving vehicles. Our insurance went through the roof. We even had trouble finding a company to cover us. But all this was only the tip of the iceberg. Underneath the surface was a much larger threat to us—the mental health of our beautiful daughter, Jessie Jean.

Jessie was always a handful. She was extremely intelligent, observant, and intuitive. It seemed she never missed a trick. Sometimes we would exchange glances that said a thousand words. Her face was so expressive that, even though she was very articulate and a great debater, she often didn't need to say a word to get her message across. She was deep, with a wisdom far beyond her years. She was creative, athletic and competitive. She was also a high achiever and would settle for nothing less than first, 100 per cent, the best.

Most people first noticed her beauty. We don't have a photo that truly does her justice. Her beauty was radiant, but a camera could not capture her inner beauty. People were drawn to her. When she blossomed into a woman, drivers narrowly escaped collisions, watching her walk down the street instead of watching the road. Guys cranked their heads almost in a full circle to watch her. She was about five feet, four inches and shapely, with a very full bosom. When left natural and long, her hair was a shining brunette with auburn highlights, thick and full of large, looping curls. She had a pixie face with eyebrows that peaked into an inverted V when she raised them at you. They rested above the most magnificent eyes, framed by long, sweeping eyelashes. Large, blue, deep and expressive, those eyes would hold you helpless in their gaze. Jessie always struggled with her identity: "Who am I? What is my purpose? Where am I going? Why am I here?" These questions seem to have haunted her since she was very young.

Her first trip to a mental health professional was in Grade 2 when she was stealing things—just little things like pencils and toys, but she knew it was wrong and it hurt people. We took her to a psychologist, who determined that she was looking for more attention from me. I felt I was giving her more than anyone, but that wasn't the point. It was how much she perceived she was getting. She was a lot of work, and I never knew what she was going to do next. She was independent, opinionated, and defiant. If she believed she was right, she would argue the point blue. Never tell Jessie that she couldn't do something; that was a challenge, and she would go about proving you wrong. She had amazing physical strength for a petite little girl and could climb anything. She had neighbours scared silly when she would shinny up the light standard in front of our house to the point where it arched, then sit and rest on the top.

Jessie Jean with a neighbour's horse, 1999. (Picture taken by Erin)

She did it on several occasions. She seemed to have to prove to herself and everyone else—especially boys—that she was as good as anyone at anything. She soaked up knowledge like a sponge and wanted to learn as much as she could about anything Dad and Clint were doing. She not only learned how to drive ATVs and snowmobiles, but she was exceptional at it at a young age. She never just sat around, and I don't recall her ever saying she was bored; she always found something to do. She liked TV, but if left to her own devices, she rarely watched it. There were usually arts and crafts supplies as an outlet for her creativity, or a book to read or a game to play. And with Erin as her best friend, cousins close by, and her beauty and outgoing personality, she always had someone to play with.

But Jessie was a fit thrower. She was the Queen of Tantrums. We never knew what would trigger one, but once it hit, it could last for one or two hours. The worst was when we were in public. I had learned through trial and error that the best way to handle the tantrum was to ignore it. If she was lying on the floor kicking and screaming and I had to go past her, I would just step over her. If I slipped and made eye contact, that would be good for another fifteen minutes of screaming and kicking. In public, I lost the advantage of being able to ignore her. A few times, the way I dealt with Jessie's fit throwing became legendary in our small town. Once, I took the kids to the arena for their skating lessons. They were at different levels, and each level was on the ice at the same time. The moms were inside having coffee, looking out the window at the kids trying to manoeuvre around pile-ons, learn a new stride, practice how to stop or skate backwards. That was when Jessie threw a fit. I don't know what started it, but there she was, in the middle of the rink, kicking away. The instructors were all kids themselves. They tried talking to her and comforting her, but nothing worked. Soon, one came in to tell me Jessie was upset and ask what they could do. I told them to ignore her. But they couldn't; they kept trying to help her. This just prolonged the event, and I could see that the entire skating program was being disrupted because of Jessie. I had to act. I told the moms I was with that I would be right back and stormed onto the ice. I didn't say a word to anyone, but grabbed Jessie's skate blades and used them like handles to skid her to the edge of the rink. I dragged her behind me so to avoid eye contact.

She was about four or five years old. She was wearing her helmet and lots of padded winter wear. At the edge of the ice, I kept walking. I dragged her along the wooden walk, up a few small steps, and right through the lobby. I didn't change pace or miss a step as I skimmed this squalling child along the floor, past the concession area to the exit door. I then picked her up, opened the nearby truck door and put her in. I removed her skates, took the keys out of the ignition and put them in my pocket. I knew her well enough to know she wouldn't want to get out of the truck in her stocking feet.

I shut the door and went back inside, sat down in the chair I had occupied earlier, and picked up my coffee. "Now," I declared, "maybe I can have my coffee in peace!" It worked. No one was there to see Jessie's fit, so what was the point of her tantrum? She was in a far better state when I went back out with Clint and Erin at the end of the session. Nothing was said about it. Nothing needed to be said. If I mentioned it, I would just get her upset again and then—boom—maybe another full-blown tantrum. She knew I wouldn't tolerate that behaviour, and that was the message I had given her without saying a word. Of course, times are different now, and I wouldn't think of leaving a child unattended in a vehicle these days, even in a small town like Beaverlodge, where everybody knows everybody else. But the ladies at the rink that day have never forgotten that episode. I hear about it yet! As Jessie got older, her tantrums diminished and her migraine headaches increased.

I always thought that Jessie was like me in a lot of ways, but she was actually more like Terry. The tantrums, however, seem to run in my side of the family. I learned that my sister's son, also creative, intelligent and competitive, was the King of Tantrums. Trying to determine where this behaviour may have originated, we discovered that

After Quadding in the mud, 1998. From left: Erin (Winkie), Raemona (Mo), Jessie Jean.

my father had been quite the tantrum-thrower when he was young. But aside from that, Jessie and Terry had a lot in common. They both suffered migraines as children. Terry grew out of his, and we hoped that Jessie would as well, but we also expected the headaches would increase in intensity as she reached puberty. They did. She would have a migraine one day and a tension headache the next, to the point where she was in physical pain every day. By this time, Jessie was in junior high school and we were living on our acreage west of Grande Prairie. This is a rough stage for a lot of kids, but it is especially hard on parents. Jessie, the consummate rebel, was very difficult. This is the stage where kids drink when they can, smoke when they can, and sneak out of the house at night. This is the phase when kids can't sleep at night, want to sleep all day, and brood in their room because no one understands them. This is when they can't find anything to wear, can't get their hair right, and think they're too fat when they aren't at all. They spend hours on the phone but have nothing to talk to a parent about. I know now that some of this behaviour is not just "normal" teenage behaviour but a symptom of depression. I have learned a lot in retrospect; I wish I had known it then. But try going through all this with constant headaches! We tried conventional medicine, but it let us down. We went to a naturopath/chiropractor who adjusted Jessie's neck and tested her for allergies. Then the practitioner put her on a strict diet to treat candida[6] and gave her some homeopathic tinctures. Six weeks on this diet seemed impossible for a teenager, but Jessie, desperate for relief, was compliant. We worked together; shopping for the right foods, trying new recipes, and within two weeks she had no more headaches. She never had another until about a month before she died. But it wasn't until 1997, when she and a friend skipped their Grade 9 classes that we found out just how bad Jessie felt about life.

On the day the girls were missing from school, Jessie's friend's mom called me about a note she found that Jessie wrote. It was frightening because it described harming herself. The hunt began. We found the

---

6   Candida is a natural yeast-like fungus that helps digestion. However, if the immune system is compromised, the beneficial candida can become a parasitic fungus known as candida albicans and can overrun the body. If the fungal infection continues unchecked, it releases toxins that can cause a variety of disorders, including digestive and bowel diseases, brain-function problems, depression and chronic fatigue syndrome.

girls and took them to the hospital, where authorities spoke to them and did a risk assessment. Jessie was admitted with suicidal ideation; her friend was sent home. We discovered later that Jessie had attempted suicide before. Erin had been there to untie the rope, to bandage the wrists. Clint had helped Jessie at a party after she passed out on pills and booze. But we knew none of this. She was a master of manipulation and made them promise not to tell. What a load to carry! And now, here was Jessie in the hospital being very uncooperative. It took several people, medication, and time before she started to improve. It took therapy with counsellors and psychiatrists, in hospital and in the outpatient's clinic, before a big turnaround.

This was when she met Dr. Madeleine Kellerman. Finally, she had someone who didn't care why she was the way she was, but just wanted to help her feel better. Jessie had found someone she could open up to, someone she respected, and someone she could trust. It was Dr. Kellerman, a young woman from South Africa, who helped Jessie understand her problem as a disease. She explained that it was her opinion that Jessie was born with a neurotransmitter problem. It upset Jessie to know that she was "defective" in some way. I helped her to understand that some people have diabetes; but this doesn't diminish them as people. I told her about celebrities I knew of with diabetes and focused on their accomplishments.

"They were born with a foul-up in their pancreas," I told her, "and they need to take insulin every day and balance what they eat with the exercise they do. They adjust to a lifestyle different from some people, but they live life to the fullest. It hasn't stopped them from achieving anything. Some folks, as in our own family—your granny, aunties, and even your dad—have thyroids that don't function properly. Without medication every day, they feel tired, can't concentrate, can't sleep properly, and a hundred other things that drag them down. Taking their pills, they can feel better and live life as they want to. You were born with brown hair, blue eyes and screwed-up neurons. You will need to take a pill every day and make some lifestyle changes in order to feel better and live life to its fullest. It doesn't take anything away from you or what you can do."

She didn't like it, but she understood and finally began to comply with her medication regime. Over time, we learned more and searched for alternative methods to improve our lives and our health. Jessie would have to change her medication a few times and still suffered side effects. One of many was horrible nightmares of blood, gore, violence, and the deaths of people she loved. She wanted to get off the pills. Our naturopath told her she needed to stay on the antidepressant Zoloft for now. Later, we learned of a doctor in the United States who was having a good response by weaning people off conventional antidepressants and on to a natural product called Sam-E[7]. We got some information from him, but he told us he couldn't help unless Jessie was under his direct care. Soon Jessie told us she felt the Zoloft wasn't working as well for controlling her depression. Our family doctor, using guidelines left by Dr. Kellerman, suggested a drug to enhance the effects of Zoloft. We suggested Sam-E. He didn't think it was available in Canada, but I told him we had some at home. We started to use Sam-E to boost the Zoloft. Then we began having Jessie take the Zoloft one day and the Sam-E the next, monitoring how she was feeling. The hope was to wean her off the Zoloft eventually; we had already managed to lower the Zoloft dosage by using the Sam-E. Not only that, but she was feeling better than ever—or so she told us. She was able to go to the Bridge Network (a store-front school) and hold down a job, which was an accomplishment for her. She was having fewer days of struggling, it seemed. She began building up the network of friends that she had before and became more socially active. The problem came when socializing involved booze. Again taking more after her dad than me, she loved beer and whisky (I can't stand the taste of either!). Alcohol is a depressant, the last thing a depressed person should take. Every time she drank, it seemed to take her a good week to ten days to balance out again. By that time, she was ready for another party. It was a vicious circle. Troubles started flaring again: difficulty concentrating on school work, not sleeping properly, lacking energy, not feeling up to going to work, not wanting to answer the

---

7   Sam-E represents a compound called S-Adenoeyl L-Methionine, a supplement formed in the body by an enzymatic reaction between adenosine-triphosphate (ATP) and methionine. It works closely with folic acid and Vitamin B12 and functions as a methyl donor. This nutrient carries and donates methyl molecules necessary to facilitate the manufacture of DNA and brain neurotransmitters. The tablets contain a compound of SamE plus folic acid, vitamin B12, and Vitamin B6.

phone. Even though we knew her mental state resulted from a disease, we found ourselves falling into the trap of treating her as if she had behavioural problems, not an illness. It's hard, though: she knew how to play on our guilt and confusion. We were at a loss as to what to do.

She was lonely, too. By this time, Erin had been at ND for her Grade 10 and went back again for Grade 11. We finally allowed Jessie's cat, Tigger, into the house as long as he stayed downstairs. She seemed to need that cat to cuddle and talk to since Winkie was away. We hounded her to pull up her socks, to act responsibly, to get her schoolwork done. She told us she was on track with school, but she wasn't. She could do amazing work, but her depression made it difficult to sustain. She fell behind and wasn't going to make the credits she needed to graduate. Being at the Bridge Network, she wasn't going to graduate with her friends at the Composite High School, but she had hoped to finish Grade 12. We told her we were proud of her effort and she could graduate another year. But though we tried to take the pressure off in some ways, she was harder on herself than we were. She applied her own pressure.

She was planning on walking with her close friend DJ (Dustin Jones) on Grad night, a plan they had had since Grade 9. DJ wanted more, but Jessie loved him as a buddy only. It was no secret, however, that DJ was so in love with her that he would wait for her until she realized that he was the one. In this, he was not unlike many guys really, except that DJ wasn't interested in any one else. DJ was special to Jessie, but Jessie was looking for her knight in shining armour. She was longing to find her man and somehow she felt that her man wasn't DJ.

She had them—her knights, people who loved her—all around her, but she couldn't see them.

I don't know what her ideal man was, but no one she knew measured up. That made her lonely and

Tigger and Jessie, December 1999.

sad. But DJ was excited about having the woman he loved by his side on graduation day, and she was looking forward to being with him and her other friends on that day.

One of the regrets I carry is the ultimatum I gave her. I did it to try to motivate her, not realizing that it wasn't motivation she needed; it was support. I refused to pay for grad pictures unless she was graduating. The last school picture I have of her is Grade 9. I so wish we had allowed her to get those pictures done. It would have made her feel better about herself, and we would have updated professional photos to add to her albums and our picture wall.

Those "woulda, shoulda, couldas" can eat you right up if you let them. Again, I was ignorant of the seriousness of her illness and saw it as attitude and behaviour problems; hindsight is always 20/20. But graduation was right around the corner. Jessie needed a dress and I was too busy to help her pick one out. She took her dad shopping with her instead. This is one of many wonderful memories that Terry has of time he spent with her. It was a beautiful dress, but needed some adjusting to fit her slender bottom and her buxom top. She took it to get alterations and she bought shoes. She changed the hair appointment that I had made because I made it for the wrong day. Soon graduation was just a week away.

The kids traditionally have a grad campout the weekend before graduation. Jessie had to work a shift on Saturday, but she had it all worked out: She would take good food with her to be sure to eat right. She took an alarm clock to get up on time so she wouldn't be late for work. She promised she would be easy on the booze and try to get enough sleep. Right! It was way too much fun to sleep, and there were so many ways to have alcohol, in jello, slushes, glasses, and bottles, and there were so many friends to drink with. Booze and veggies don't go down as well as booze and hot dogs, and of course when you drink you smoke. Who can sleep when the party is raging? You might miss something good. You can always sleep after the weekend is over. Needless to say, all those good intentions ran afoul. I remember going grocery shopping with her for the campout. She ran over to the fruits and asked me, "Please Mom, can we buy some plums? I love these kinds of plums!" I of course bought her some. The trick to eating right is to make sure that the food that is good for you is food that you like. To this day I can't pass by plums without thinking of her, and on occasion I find myself getting weepy—over plums! You never know what will tug at your heart-strings. Anything can twig a memory when you least expect it. I often wonder if she actually ate her plums. She didn't have them when she came home, so I suppose she did.

She was tired that Monday morning and didn't want to get out of bed. She also had contracted a nasty bladder infection and was experiencing a lot of discomfort. She hadn't gone to work that weekend and now was not planning on going again as she was ill, but she didn't have the courtesy to call and let her employer know. Terry and I were infuriated! What we realize now is that courtesy, maturity, and responsibility had nothing to do with it. It was about depression and her inability to make the call and speak to her employer.

At the time, however, Terry told me I better handle this issue with her because he was too upset. I went downstairs and talked to Jessie. I tried to get her to call her boss. I used every technique I could think of. I finally lost my temper and blew up at her. I told her I was giving her five minutes to pick up the phone and call. That didn't work either. I was beside myself with fury and frustration; she didn't say a word. After I had my temper tantrum, I realized I was missing the point and perhaps needed to give in because she was ill. I still didn't recognize

Grad Campout May 20, 2000. From left: Brittany, Jody, Jessie.

her mental illness as the culprit. I focused on the physical. I made an appointment for her to see the doctor on Tuesday. She didn't go, and of course she never called to cancel. She also never picked up the phone when we called from work to check on her.

That evening I spoke with her again. This time I was trying to persuade her to see a doctor. By now, she was running a fever, but she had no faith in doctors. She wanted to know if she could just take some herbs and supplements to fix her up. I explained that herbs are great things. In combination with good eating habits, exercise, and proper sleep, herbs can help build up immune systems, balance hormones, support organ function, and accomplish a host of other things. But when an infection is already full-blown, you need aggressive treatment. I explained that she needed antibiotics or she would just get worse and she would be in no shape for graduation. After she finished her antibiotic treatment, we could put her on some acidophilus and some red clover to boost her immune system, clean her blood and get some good digestive bacterial balance happening.

"What will they do?" she asked, referring to the hospital staff. I told her that they would ask questions, take her temperature, pulse and such, maybe take a urine sample, tell her they think she is has a bladder infection, then prescribe some antibiotics. "The sooner we do this, the faster you can start feeling better," I told her. But it was late before I finally got her into the car and into the emergency room at the Queen Elizabeth II Hospital in Grande Prairie. It was hours before they saw her. They did everything I said they would and gave her some painkillers as well as antibiotics, with a prescription for both. By the time we got home, it was late. I encouraged Jessie to take her pills, but she was very reluctant. She had learned how hard on your liver Tylenol and other pills are after she took a handful of Tylenol and learned that her liver was stressed. I was thankful that she had no permanent damage. She seemed very concerned about her health and very particular about what went into her body. I was glad she asked questions and wanted the best for herself, but she still couldn't accept the detrimental effect alcohol had on her physical and mental health. I felt that would come in time if she cared so much for her health. We talked about that and about the rough time I gave her over not phoning her boss. We stood in the kitchen hugging as we talked. Clint and Terry were already in bed. We rocked in each other's arms. I smelled her hair and kissed her head. I told her I was going to head for Edmonton early in the morning and I was travelling with some other women. I said I would leave the address where she could pick up the car. We were still rocking and I rubbed her back as we cuddled. Could she fill the dishwasher while I was gone so Dad didn't have to look at dirty dishes the whole time I was away?

"If you're lucky!" she said, and looked at me with those pixie eyes that shone with mischief and humour. I said I'd be home around suppertime on Thursday. We held on a while longer. She said, "I love you 'melly bum," using a term of affection that was unique to her. "I love you more," I piped back as we played our usual game. "Nope, I love you more," she replied. "Nope, I love you more," I came back. "Nope," she said with a lilt. I told her I had to get to sleep as I was leaving around six in the morning. "Good night, sweetness," I said. "Good night, momma" she returned. I left her in the kitchen and went to bed.

On Thursday, I started our five-hour trip home from Edmonton with the three women I was travelling with. There had been a meeting that morning that two of the women had attended, so we left around noon.

We would be getting home around five o'clock. My cell phone rang and it was my secretary. She wanted to speak with one of the other women. I didn't really think much of it as our office had done business with her and there had been a mix-up with an invoice at one point. I thought maybe another bit of that business needed clearing up. I didn't know it then, but my secretary told my friend Linda that they were to bring me straight to the office. There was an urgent family matter but she was not to let on that anything was going on. Linda was perfect. She never dropped a hint. I had no clue. She asked to be dropped off at the Golden Star restaurant to meet her husband. That establishment was directly across from my office. So I said that would be perfect for me, too. As we approached, I told them they could park in our building's lot as it would be easier to unload bags there than on the street. As we came up to the lot, I saw Clint's truck and Terry standing by it. My first thought was that he had borrowed Clint's truck for some reason and had learned through Linda's husband, Rod, that we would be arriving there, and he was there as a surprise to pick me up. I was glad I wouldn't have to wait for him and we could head right home. But as we pulled in to park, I saw Clint. Then I saw another vehicle parked there, and Peter stepped out. I knew Peter from Beaverlodge several years earlier when he was stationed there as an RCMP officer. We got out of the car and I said to the ladies, "I think I'm about to get some bad news." I got my bags out of the back and Peter approached me. "We have to talk, is there somewhere inside where we could sit down?" I unlocked and went inside. We went into one of the classrooms and he set out a chair for me to sit in, one for Terry, who hadn't said a word so far, to sit next to me, and one for him to sit facing us. Clint paced around beside and behind us. I don't recall the exact words, but I remember his saying that it was about Jessie. I had already figured that out, and it really wasn't a big surprise. What *was* a shock were his next words. There had been an incident. And no, Jessie was not okay; Jessie was dead.

Was I breathing? Did I hear that? Is this real? Somebody hold on to me so I don't sink into the floor or float to the roof. I didn't feel as if I was in this place. I was numb. And it got worse.

The fact that she killed herself, she had used a gun, and Clint had found her—all these points felt like knives stabbing into my already bleeding chest. I felt Clint's hand on my shoulder, and I was squeezing Terry's hand. I broke into a sobbing puddle, not knowing what to say or do next. I remember that the door opened and there was Terry's mom Vi, Uncle Willy, and my sisters-in-law. Family was gathering and I held on to them all, not wanting to let go for fear I would not be able to stand up without them.

My family was my next thought. Peter said someone from the Beaverlodge detachment was going to head over to Curtis and Laurie's to let them know. So my brother would know—what about my sisters? I needed to tell them. I left the room to head back to the office, and there stood Gail, my secretary, and Jennifer, her assistant. They had just learned the horrible news. I stopped to hug them. Then there were Linda, Sharon and Helen, the women I had travelled with. They were in shock as well, especially Linda, whose sons were friends with Jessie and Clint. We had known Linda and Rod for some time as they had grown up in Beaverlodge, too. I found a phone and called my sister Marilyn. She is the youngest, but I knew she was very close to Jessie, a kindred spirit. I had to tell her first. Could she call the others? Heather and Lee Ann lived with their families in Vancouver. Marilyn and her boys lived in Duncan on Vancouver Island.

We went from my office to Patsy and George's house. Patsy had been divorced from Bob for a while. It had been bitter, and the settlement was not yet final, but she had found happiness with a new partner, George, and they shared a house in Grande Prairie. People started showing up: friends, more family, and Jessie's friends. Food and flowers started to arrive, too. I couldn't tell you who came and when; it is all a blur. We stayed there that night and several nights after.

That Thursday morning had been a good one for Terry. He had spoken with Jessie the night before as she sat doing homework in the basement in front of the TV. He had told her his plans for the next day and asked how she was feeling. He asked if she had been in his closet, as he was missing a sweater. He had said good night. He usually checked on her in the morning too, but he looked down the stairs, as he was getting ready to leave the house and noticed the mattress in the doorway. There is no door at the bottom of the stairs, but a foam mattress we owned fit the space well, covering the entrance to the staircase and keeping Tigger out of our upstairs realm. Terry assumed she was probably sleeping soundly and decided not to bother her. He would be back early in the afternoon and could check on her then. Clint had gone to his summer job, where he usually got his lunch break at one and often came home for lunch. He would fly through the door and charge down stairs to find Jessie sitting on the couch watching music videos and doing her school work. They would talk a bit—and he would no doubt tease and torment her a bit—then he'd make himself a sandwich and head back to work.

This day was different. He didn't find her on the couch, but on the floor in a pool of blood. He called 9-1-1 and did cardio-pulmonary rescusitation (CPR), but she had known what she was doing. It had been quick; she wasn't coming back. It wasn't long before the yard at our once-peaceful acreage was swarming with activity—police cars with lights churning, officers invading our home, an ambulance sitting in the yard. DJ drove by. He had come to visit Jessie and find out what colour her dress was so he could buy her an appropriate corsage. He was sent home but told nothing. Clint phoned Terry, who was having lunch with colleagues in town. He was home in a flash. He must have had a million emotions and thoughts flooding through his mind and his heart. He was upset at the way his home was no longer under his control, but was the scene of a police investigation. Cops tried stopping him from going in. They tried stopping him at the top of the stairs. It was Clint who met his dad and convinced him not to go downstairs. It was Clint who was strong and in control while anger and pain tore Terry from the inside out. After the initial shock, they still had to prepare to tell me. They didn't know how I would react, especially since she had used a gun—they knew I didn't like guns. They had hours to wait until I was home. Peter was amazing: as a friend and as a police officer; he was compassionate and understanding but did his job professionally. We know that was hard on him and took its toll on his emotions, but he was there for us and knew just what to do and what to say. Thank God for Peter LeBlanc. Now I knew, my siblings knew, Terry's family all knew. But we had to tell Winkie, and she was in Saskatchewan. We arranged to have Erin be joined by her house parent, mentor (another teacher), and the priest while she was on the phone with us. I remember Terry and me sitting on Patsy's deck telling her over the phone that her sister, a part of her heart, had died. The school arranged to fly her home accompanied by her house parent. At the layover in Calgary, they ran into Dillon, her cousin, who was also flying home.

We spent the night at Patsy and George's. Friday morning, when we woke up, I remember thinking: damn, it isn't all a dream; it's real. Terry and I lay staring at the ceiling and talking, trying to make sense of it all, trying to understand how we were feeling and what we would do now. That day I wanted to go out to the house. I needed some fresh clothes and I needed a scrapbook that Jessie had put together for her compulsory "Career and Life Management" high school course. It was and still is an amazing keepsake. We decided that my sister-in-law, Jackie, would stay with me and drive me wherever I wanted to go. She was incredible: she knew just when to speak and what to say; she knew when to say nothing. She never told me that this or that was a bad idea or judged me in any way. I will be eternally grateful for her grace and wisdom on that day. She was exactly who and what I needed. I recall going to the house. My brother Curtis, Terry's cousin Darryl, Terry, and his brother Roy were there. I can't remember whom else. They had been patching up the holes where the bullet had gone through and removed the bloodstained carpeting, replacing it with a new patch.

I remember standing in the kitchen by the telephone and as I looked down I noticed a small tear in the linoleum. Jackie noticed me staring at it trying to figure out what it was. She had tried to keep me from seeing it, but now she looked at me helplessly as the realization moved through my mind and across my face.

"Is that . . .?" I started to say while seeing in Jackie's eyes that it was exactly what I thought it was. The guys hadn't gotten to this repair yet. It was the hole where the bullet had gone through the ceiling downstairs where Jessie had shot herself and up through the kitchen floor finally coming to rest in the vaulted ceiling in the kitchen. My eyes were riveted on that hole in the floor. It pulled me toward it as I imagined the path the bullet had taken. I placed my fingers on it and wept.

Jackie lifted me up and embraced me giving me the comfort and support I needed. Some family and friends had also been in the house doing housework.

A neighbour, Georgina, had been out in the yard mowing our four acres for us. We found ourselves surrounded by love and engulfed in acts of love. People said we were so strong, but it was all their love that gave us our strength. When we returned to Patsy's, Jessie's friends started showing up. They came to be with us and to see Erin, who had just arrived. They had just come from the grand march rehearsal for graduation tomorrow. DJ sat on a footstool in the living room. I sat down, put my arm around him, and asked him how he was, if he was okay. I asked whom he was going to walk with in the grand march, and he said he didn't know, maybe with Raemona and her escort. I looked over at Erin, sandwiched on the couch between friends of Jessie and her. I thought out loud, "To bad Erin couldn't do it." I didn't see the wordless interaction between them. I was soon talking with someone else and looked over to see Terry sit down next to DJ, put his arm around him and ask him the same things I had. Only this time when he asked whom DJ would be walking with, DJ answered, "Your other daughter, if she wants to." Terry was shocked, not knowing about my comments, and Erin looked over to DJ and nodded yes. Well, the house was abuzz.

We have to find Winkie a dress, shoes, and a hairdo. All at once we had something else to think about, something to work toward. Soon Erin had a selection of dresses to try on. She wanted to look good, but not to outshine the grads.

"I can't look like I'm graduating and take anything away from them" she insisted. Soon she had her dress, though it needed adjusting. That was okay because Dawn Calvert was on the stairs with a needle and thread, tape measure and scissors, making sure the dress fit perfectly.

It was so appropriate. Dawn lived across the street from us when we lived in Beaverlodge, and she babysat my kids when I worked for the ambulance service. The kids spent so much time at her house that Erin used to call her "Mom" and me "Momma." Now she was doing alterations on Erin's dress. Looking back, getting Erin ready to go to the Grand March graduation ceremonies was a pleasant distraction. Clint, through all this, spent time with his male cousins and some of his friends. He kept busy and active, golfing mostly, another sweet distraction that gave him what he needed to work through his grief.

The next day we continued to have visitors and were making arrangements for a service. My sisters and a niece were on their way and would stay at our house on the acreage when they arrived. Auntie Lorraine started doing Winkie's hair and cousin Carolyn helped with her makeup. The dress was done, the shoes fit, and Erin was ready. I got ready to go, too. There was no way we were going to miss this graduation grand march! The kids all wanted us there, and we weren't about to let them down. Terry was at our house, where dear friends from Spirit River had arrived to pay their respects. He was going to be a bit late. Linda and Rod Dunbar had a son, Lanny, who was graduating, and they offered to take us with them. Soon there was a knock at the door and there stood DJ. He looked sharp in his tux and held a corsage in his hand. He slipped it onto Erin's wrist. We had them pose for several pictures for us.

He asked me to follow them outside, where he presented Erin with the gift that he had bought for Jessie. He wanted Erin to have it now. It was a fine silver bracelet with a delicate, silver, heart pendant on it. He struggled with the clasp but was determined to put it on Erin himself. She looked stiff and unsure of each step on her new high heels as

DJ escorted her to his car. I had my fingers crossed that she wouldn't trip or catch a heel on the stairs they would be descending. I hoped she knew what she was doing and would be strong enough to carry this out. I prayed that Dustin could make it through, too, because I knew he was fragile under his steady-as-a-rock exterior. Terry made it a bit later and was ready to go by the time the Dunbars showed up. I clung to a box of Kleenex I had with me. The grand march was held in the Canada Games Arena, the bleachers full of families, friends and well-wishers of all the graduates. Soon the announcements came as to what we could expect. Only the graduates' names would be called. If a female grad walked with a non-grad, her name followed by "and escort" would be read. If a male grad was walking with a non-graduate, then we could expect to hear his name followed by "and friend." Grads were coming out in alphabetic order, and Rod told us he would photograph whomever we wished. As grads started to appear, stand on stage, descend the stairs and circle the floor, we noticed that most of them were wearing yellow ribbons. Jessie's friend, Nathan Lamoureux, had lost his brother to suicide only a few years earlier. His family became very active in the Yellow Ribbon Light for Life Foundation promoting suicide prevention and offering kids ways to ask for help. The ribbons identified support for suicide prevention. It was beautiful to see them doing this in honour and remembrance of Jessie. We asked Nathan and his older sister to speak on the Light for Life Foundation at Jessie's memorial service. We started to see kids we knew. They were beautiful and charming, beaming and shining. Each one that knew us looked for us in the stands and gave us a smile or a wave. Then it came. We were expecting to hear "Dustin Jones and friend," but instead we heard, "Dustin Jones and Erin Atkinson in memory of her sister, Jessie." This was highly irregular. Jessie not only was not graduating; she didn't even go to the school. Erin and DJ told me later that when Erin asked the announcer to read it that way, he initially refused. Erin was very insistent and persuasive, however, and the announcement was made. They walked on stage. Erin had her head held high, glowing radiant beams from her face. She floated down the stairs and, arm in arm; she and DJ walked across the floor. I could barely see through my tears. She told me later that she knew Jessie was with her, that she was proud to be able to walk with Jessie's friends for her, and that is where she found her strength. I was in awe. My box of Kleenex was a soggy lump on my lap. I couldn't speak. I was sobbing uncontrollably. My tears were filled with extreme sorrow and extreme joy—a mix of so many emotions that I just couldn't bear it. They were such a gorgeous couple. When their names were announced, a huge cheer filled the arena. People rose to their feet and applauded. Many eyes shot our direction. Erin and Dustin couldn't walk two steps without having to stop to get their picture taken.

When they finished their promenade, Nathan took Erin for a walk around the floor while Dustin took Brittany, who had been on Nathan's arm. All were dear friends of Jessie, and all were sharing special feelings with each other and with us. We saw them all and we were proud of them all. Afterward, we came down out of the stands to be close to the kids before they commenced with the evening. We saw them looking up in the stands where we had been and, not seeing us there, they looked upset and desperately scanned the arena for us. We joined their little circle and they were glad to see us. We told them how wonderful they all were. We each told them that they were to go and have fun that night. Tonight was theirs. They had earned it and they deserved it. Jessie would be with them in spirit. They needed to know that it was okay to celebrate this moment of achievement in their lives, even though they were grieving the loss of a friend. It was as if they had to have permission from us, and we gladly gave it. Those kids mean the world to us—Raemona, DJ, Brittney, Nathan, Jody, Lanny, the whole gang! It gave us a sense of purpose to be there for them, and being allowed to share in this major event made us feel that life still held joy in the light of the life in each of these precious souls.

I remember Terry asking the morning after we lost Jessie, as we lay there still trying to understand what had happened, "What did we do wrong?"

I replied, "How can you think we did anything wrong? Look at Erin and Clinton and how they are. This isn't about us. We raised three exceptional, beautiful, charming, intelligent, wonderful people. We should be proud of that. This was about Jessie, her depression, and her inability to cope. Not us."

I thought of this again as we received the tearful smiles and warm hugs from those kids as they went off into the night to celebrate graduation. We allowed Erin to go to the party, too. It would be a "safe grad," which meant that there would be booze, but the party would be restricted to graduates and their guests, and they would be at a "secret" location to which they would be bussed. There would be food, discrete adult supervision, and first aid available. We figured that Erin would be safer this night at this wild party than when she was in my own womb! Every soul there would treat her with nothing but respect and admiration. She would have all these people looking out for her. She missed her "curfew" but we weren't worried. She had fun and we were happy that she had that wonderful distraction.

Are there things worse than death? Some can create a reality for themselves that is much worse than death. It is an agonising existence. They see no point in life; find no joy, and suffer emotional and spiritual pain every day. Some choose to die rather than to die piece by piece, little by little, every day they are alive. They choose an end to it. It is so sad; it is tragic. I weep and my heart breaks when I think about the pain and hopelessness my beautiful little girl endured. I feel guilt that I didn't understand it and wasn't as empathetic as I could have been. I wasn't there for her when she needed me.

I didn't hear what she was saying—not really. This is the source of my greatest pain, my guilt and regret. I tried to express my grief. I wrote it out on my computer and saved it as "griefvent.doc" It is dated June 19th, 2000, less than a month after losing Jessie. I share it with you now.

Nathan Lamoureux and Dustin Jones (DJ), getting ready to go to the after-graduation party, May 27, 2000.

CHAPTER EIGHT

Venting

JUNE 19, 2000

I t's strange what the mind does when you mourn. She would be exactly eighteen years and four months old today. I knew her twelve days longer than I knew my parents. It's a year since Carmen Willis was shot on Trickle Creek Farm. That was the night of our Lakeview Party, the night Jessie and a friend snuck away and went missing, the night that started a chain of events that led to lessons learned the hard way: leaving home, going to Vancouver Island alone, adventures and relationships, a few hours at the police station and the betrayal of a friend. This was just one sequence of life lessons that helped Jessie become the beautiful young woman she was. There were many, but I only know of those in which I was involved in some way. Her life was so complex, so full of love and yet so tortured.

It's been said—as I already knew—that time will heal. Time took the edge off my grief when I lost my parents, yet I still miss them after twenty-six years and weep for them once in a while when I wish they could share in my life's "occasions."

I think that is what I fear now. What if I don't want the edge taken off my grief? I don't want to forget her scent, her face, the touch of her clammy little hand, her warm cuddly hugs, the sound of her voice and her giggle. I don't want time to dim the images of her that I see clearly now but feel are already slipping away. Those expressive eyes flashing me mischief, wonder, wisdom, understanding, humour. Those casual glances were connections, the golden threads linking our souls. More than a daughter, she was so much a part of me that her loss leaves me feeling maimed—as if a vital organ had been ripped out of my body. How can I live without her? Differently—I will never be the same.

She told me more than once that she felt she would not live to see her twentieth birthday. She said she didn't know why; it was just a strong feeling she had. "No, please don't talk like that," I said. "I can't imagine living without you." But I, too, had that haunting feeling. I ignored it, pushed it away; it's just my imagination and I won't acknowledge it. Is eighteen years long enough to live, long enough to know someone, long enough?

Thankfully, I now look back with few regrets. She had love and adventure and wonderful life experiences. I wish she could have had more. But she also had horrible sadness and despair. I couldn't begin to understand. How could I have known the depth of her pain? How could I understand the torture of getting up and facing each day and the agony of trying to make each day count without hurting anyone around her? But she did it. Eighteen years is a long time to endure pain, a long time to be dying.

Many lives have been touched by this precious soul, and many continue to be touched. She mattered. Her life and her death have meant something, have left an impression on this world. She has taught us to treasure life, family, and friends. She has reminded us that love is the only thing that really matters and that it should flow from us freely, radiating beams to touch everyone we meet. What I have learned is that depression is an illness, a disease. I heard these words before, but I wasn't truly listening. Now I finally get it. So do a lot of other people.

Imagine a child with cancer. We have research, societies, foundations, agencies, and service groups that pull together to support children suffering from this often-terminal disease. Our hearts bleed when we see the smiling face of a child swollen from treatment, hairless from chemotherapy and radiation. We marvel at the strength of this tiny, brave soul, fighting through the pain to stay positive and cheerful each day of the struggle. The pain is obvious; we can see it. We are inspired by the courage of this little person—so young, too young to have to suffer so. We reach into ourselves and put what we can into trying to support the fight to stamp out this horrible plague.

Imagine another child with depression. The pain is hidden: We see a perfect bright smile; we see a healthy body, strong and beautiful, shining locks of gorgeous hair, sparkling eyes. And when she can't get out of bed, she is lazy and we have to force her up and get her motivated. When we see her schoolwork suffer, we discipline. When she can't seem to even help around the house with a few chores, she's being lazy again. When she isolates herself in her room, she's being antisocial, a typical teenager: rebellious, lazy, stays up all night and wants to sleep all day. But this one is special. She's depressed. She's been a handful for some time, and now we know why. Well, we can fix that. She has lots of love and support. With medication and counselling, if we try hard enough, she'll get better. And she has some good days, so she must be okay. We'll get through this together.

But we miss the point. Inside she is suffering horribly. The disease is eating her up. Each day is a struggle for survival. Only now, after the disease took control and she lost her battle, do we see her courage—and we are in awe. How could someone so young and seemingly so fragile have the strength to get through each day doing her best to be cheerful and think of others, as she did? We are inspired. Life has to matter. Life shouldn't have to be a struggle every day. We need to do something to make a change, to make our lives count. Just like a cancer, depression can beat you, or you can beat it. Unlike cancer, depression does not conjure up empathy, funding for research, or public awareness. We don't want to share our depression-survival story as we do our cancer-survival story. No one wants to hear how you suffered a mental illness and just made it through. We'd rather hear about the surgery that removed your cancer and the brutal radiation and chemical treatments that obliterated it from your by now devastated body.

Cancer can be beaten; we know that slogan well. Depression can be beaten, too, but first we need to acknowledge it as the terrible disease that it is. You can be depressed for many reasons, but sometimes the only reason is that you were born that way. No event changed you; you just have something biologically "off." Your resistance is down. You're at high risk for losing the battle.

I feel as if I need to get this lesson—which I learned the hard way—to as many people as I can. It's okay to grieve for someone who lost control to their disease, whether it be cancer, diabetes, heart disease, or depression.

It seems that I always need a soapbox and a cause to preach about. This is who I am. I placed my focus on other areas of safety and health care because I didn't quite understand about suicide. I just remember vividly my mother looking at me one day with a far off gaze and a slightly wistful smile.

"What?" I asked.

"Oh, you sometimes remind me of my Uncle Norman," she replied.

I didn't even know I had a great-uncle named Norman. She told me that I wouldn't. He shot himself when she was only 16. She told me with bitterness and anger that he had been her favourite uncle and had done this terrible, selfish, cowardly thing. She cursed him for it, especially when, for weeks and months afterwards, she would still find traces of blood as she was cleaning the bathroom where he had used the shotgun on himself. I remember so clearly her anger and sorrow. I remember that it was a family secret, never to be spoken of. It would be too shameful to acknowledge this abhorrent event. So I never heard about this uncle before. And I never learned why he had once been my Mom's favourite uncle.

I remember telling Jessie about how selfish an act suicide was—partly because that is what I had been taught, and partly because I hoped somehow that she wouldn't consider suicide again, as she was trying to be so considerate of other people's feelings.

She made an audio recording before she died. She let us all know how she loved us and that she knew how much she was loved.

"Don't blame yourselves," she said. "I know you will, but don't. This isn't your fault; it's all me." She kept saying over and over, "I'm sorry; please forgive me." She said she knew what a selfish act this was. I heard many of my words come back at me through her little speech on that recording. That suicide was a selfish act was only one of my own impressions that was reflected back on me.

My pain is so deep that I can't find words to tell you how much I hurt. Yet I could never take my own life. I thought that it was because I valued it too much as a precious gift from God, and that to treat it badly or destroy it would be the ultimate blasphemy. But now I know it is because the pain I feel now is but a tiny drop compared to the ocean of pain my sweet child lived with every day. My grief arises not only because she is gone—and because of my own selfish feelings of wanting her back for *me* to hold, *me* to comfort—but also because she suffered so. My child hurt and I couldn't take the pain away; I couldn't make it better. That is my job. I'm the mom. I kiss the hurts and make them go away. I cradle the hurt children in my arms and tell them, "It's okay, Mommy is here; nothing can hurt you now." I would wrestle a charging bear, jump into a raging river—anything, anything to save my children. But I couldn't take her pain away.

I know. She's okay now, at peace, with God. I have no doubt. But that isn't the point. I feel as if I failed her. I know I shouldn't, but I do. And she's gone forever. My life will never again be the same. Say she's okay now a million times and it won't change that. It won't take my pain away.

I see her friends mourn for her. I see the grief in all those people whose lives she touched. I feel I need to be there for them; it's the caregiver in me.

And then there is my wonderful son Clint and my baby girl, Erin—both amazing. I want to help them with their pain as they try to help me with mine, so I worry about them and try to be strong for them. I thank God every day for the wondrous blessings I have been given. My children are three of my greatest gifts. My husband is another of the amazing blessings I have been granted.

His pain is something I can almost taste. We share the same bitter dish but also share the sweetness. Thank God for him. But I try not to cry too much. I try to stay positive and supportive for his sake. He needs me now more than ever, and I can't let him down. I need him, too, but I always have, and I have always taken his love for granted. He has always been there for me—for us. Now he has been shaken to his toes. My rock has crumbled. We are now both fine sand. Only by staying together and using our love to bind us will we form that solid, strong unit that we need to be. The combined shattered parts of ourselves will act as a foundation to build our lives on again, so we need to find the strength to make it as strong and sound a foundation as possible. Right now we are blowing in the wind. It is the love of our family, our friends, and the prayers of the community—people we don't even know—that provide the glue we need to make it through each day.

It seems that whatever we need, we get it just when we need it the most. A phone call, a prayer, a letter, a song, a butterfly, the blossoming of a rose, a card, a visit, a hug, rain, and sunshine.

God is with us; we are sure of that. He's in the love that surrounds us and wells up within us.

I don't know what comes after this life: reincarnation, another dimension, Heaven, or more choices. Do we get to be angels or do we keep coming back until we get it right, and then get placed on high? I don't know. I just know that this life is only part of it all, and I don't want to live it in the dark. But right now, I'm tired, so tired. Every day I wake up and wish that I would wake up all the way and find that all this was just a dream. Instead, I have to try to make the day count. It takes a lot of effort right now, especially when all I want to do is say: "Time Out. Can we start again? I want to set the clock back and begin again. I'll savour each minute more intensely this time. I'll etch every look into my mind. I'll slow each touch down to make it last longer so it is felt with my whole soul, not just my arms or my fingertips. I'll study her every move as if it will be the last time I ever get to see it. I'll hang on every word. Please?"

So I try to do that now with Terry, Clint and Erin. But it's hard. I'll smother them if I hang on too tight. I guess the best I can do is carry on with life as best I can. I must have done something right to have so many friends who love me, to have a soul mate whom I love more each day, and to have raised my children to be the caring, wonderful people they are. I'll just try to radiate love more brightly and wrap myself around each moment with more intensity.

Butterflies are just little bugs; rainbows are just light refracting off water drops; roses are just thorny bushes trying to thrive. But it is through our eyes and our experiences that these things hold meaning. Rainbows may hold the meaning of God's promise of eternal love, or they may remind you of other things, too. A rose may symbolize love, or it may remind you of someone or some event. A butterfly may represent the promise of eternal life. But it also may prompt remembrance of someone you love, flying as free through the air as a spirit, touching you as its delicate wings carry it through the turbulent currents, spreading life from flower to flower and reminding you of how powerful an effect a tiny, fragile life can have on the world.

JESSIE'S WORDS

These next few inserts are things that Jessie wrote. I have included them to help you understand what a person with depression feels like. She wrote so well that you can feel her pain. I wonder, if I had read the February 15, 2000, letter to her sister, whether I would have recognized how serious her condition was. Honestly, I don't think so. I would have recognized the pain of loneliness and known she was deeply blue, but I wouldn't have been aware of the suicide risk this letter seems to indicate. Knowing what I know now, I would have spoken to her right away if I had read the letter. I would have told her she sounded very sad. I would have asked her if she had been thinking of killing herself. We could have spoken about it, worked through it, sought professional help—and maybe averted her untimely death.

I see now that her death has led me to understand what I didn't know then. Her death has prompted me to speak to young people in schools and teach them how to get help, how to recognize when a friend is in trouble, and how to help that friend. Jessie's death has sent me on a journey of personal growth and renewed purpose. I know that it was in her living and her dying that so many people have grown in positive ways. Good has come out of tragedy. Therefore, I share these writings of hers with you so that you may learn now what I wish I had known then. I believe Jessie's death had purpose, and part of that may have been to lead me to help others overcome their depression and to prevent others from dying by their own hand. If you read this and see that this is how someone you love feels, then maybe you can act quickly to save them. Recognizing the risk of suicide can sometimes save lives. If one person can be lifted out of the depths through the help of a caring soul who found understanding and guidance in what Jessie and I have written, then our lives have been worth living in this world.

The first letter was e-mailed from my office computer on Clinton's 20th birthday. Jessie probably had sent him a birthday greeting via e-mail and then sent her sister a quick note as well. At this time, Clint was playing Junior A hockey for the Athol Murray College of Notre Dame in Wilcox, Saskatchewan, and Erin was attending Grade 10 at Notre Dame. Clint was billeted with a family there and Erin was living in the dorms. We were planning to go to see them in March for the "Mother–Daughter" weekend. Jessie and I would stay in the dorm with Erin, and Terry was going to stay at the Kaips', where Clint was billeted. We would be able to take in some hockey and spend quality time with each other. Jessie wrote of some things happening in her life and tells of her sadness.

From: Faris Atkinson <fatkinson@stjohn.ab.ca>
To: Erin Atkinson <ATKINSONE@notredame.sk.ca>
Sent: Tuesday, February 15, 2000 6:07 pm

Subject: Hidey Ho!

Well I am using mom's computer right now to write to you, but the internet will be set up at home soon. It turns out that dad doesn't like it at the 214 Place, so he moved all his stuff back home. I miss you so much doodle bug! I wrote you a letter and mailed it today, so you should be getting it soon.

On Friday night, Nathan came over with a movie (Pulp Fiction) and he snuggled up to me on the couch. It was very crazy. He doesn't think that it is too weird to get cozy with his ex while he's going out with some one. Yes, him and Jen are still together. He took her out on Valentines day, and then had the nerve to ask me who I was with on Valentines, when he knows damn well that I am not with anyone. I kinda wish I was though.

I read the e-mail that you

Winkie and Jessie at the Mother Daughter Weekend at Notre Dame, March 2000. This is the last weekend they spent together.

wrote mom, and I had to giggle because you are just too precious for words. That is pretty cool about Carolyn hey? Auntie Patsy is going to be a grandma! Mom and dad are going to be 'Great Auntie' and 'Great Uncle'. Weird.

I can hardly wait to come and see you and Clint. I miss you both so much.

I think that I will call you tonight. Yes I think I will. I haven't been myself these past couple of days. It just seems that lately I have realized that I may not graduate this year, and I just want to give up. I'm sorry I don't want you to worry about me, but I just feel like some one is holding my head under-water, with his foot pressing down on my chest, and only letting the grip loosen enough for me to get short gasps of air. I feel stuck, and helpless.

Anyway, I should go because mom is waiting for me. I'm sorry that this news isn't the greatest, and I know it's not what you want to hear. I love you, and I'm always thinking about you. I just wish that you could be here right now so that I could hug you, and just let out all my tears. You know that feeling that you get in your throat when you're going to cry? I have that all the time. I just can't seem to cry enough to make it go away.

I gotta go now. I love you SOOOOOOOOOOOOOOOO much.

Love Jessie

If, as you read this letter from Jessie, you said to yourself that you feel the same way right now as she did when she wrote it, you need to talk to some one right away that can help you. Do not delay. Please call a crisis line, a help line, or speak to a counsellor. Turn to Appendix "H" in the back of this book for resources if you don't know where to start. There is help. We care about you.

The next letter is a transcript of a suicide note that Jessie wrote to Erin. I think she wrote it first and then decided to make the audiotape.

Erin,

Please forgive me, I'm so sorry for leaving you. I'm just not strong enough. I was going nowhere in my life, and too scared to do anything about it. But you're strong, and you can get through this. You're going to be wonderful in whatever you do. You're going to grow up, get married, have kids, and grandkids, and you'll become your dreams.

You are the best sister anyone could have, and I am thankful I had you as mine. Nothing was ever the same when you were away from home. Eating, watching T.V., getting ready to go out somewhere, cleaning, getting ready for bed, and getting up in the morning. Brushing my hair wasn't even the same without you sitting next to me saying how disgusting it was how much hair falls out of my head. Sleeping wasn't even the same. Everything seems so much stranger when you're not here sharing it with me. Now, it is me leaving you, and for this I couldn't be more sorry. It hurts me so much to know how sad you will be.

I love you Winkie, and never forget that no matter what, you will still be able to talk to me, and I will always be able to hear you.

Tell Nathan that I love him and need his forgiveness as well. Be strong for him, Erin. He's been through a lot of deaths and needs your strength.

Please tell D.J. that he has been a huge part of my life and I love him so much. Ask him to forgive me for my actions.

Both Nathan and D.J. have had such a huge impact and made so much difference in my life. They both have always held a special place in my heart. Let them know that.

Tell Clint that I need his forgiveness. Tell him and Mom and Dad that I love them dearly and I'm sorry. I know Clint is smart and he will make the perfect decision, the best decision for *him* and his future.

Winkalicious, you don't know how much I wish that I could have given you one last hug and snuggle. Just to rub my cheek to yours, and smell you. I miss your smell. God, I pray that you will be all right. I love you more than anything. I love you so much that my heart hurts to think what I will be putting you through. Just remember that this was my choice, and I will be happy. I will be with God and Grandpa. I'll be happy.

Don't forget to talk to me[8].

Sometimes, Erin, you'll see me in your dreams and hear my voice in your heart. I'll always be in you, with you, and I'll always listen for you to say my name, and fill me in on the details of your life. I know that this won't be easy to get over, but in time your heart will heal, and you will smile again. Don't give up like I did. Never give up. I love you.

Love, Your sister and best friend,

Jessie Jean

---

8   Jessie Jean wrote this line in large letters for emphasis. See original letter.

Erin,

Please forgive me, I'm so sorry for leaving you. I'm just not strong enough. I was going nowhere in my life, and to scared to do anything about it. But you're strong, and you can get through this. You're going to be wonderful in whatever you do. You're going to grow up, get married, have kids, and grandkids, and you'll become your dreams.

You are the best sister anyone could have, and I am thankfull I had you as mine. Nothing was ever the same when you were away from home. Eating, watching t.v, getting ready to go out somewhere, cleaning, getting ready for bed, and getting up in the morning. Brushing my hair wasn't even the same without you sitting next to me saying how disgusting it was how much hair falls out of my head. Sleeping wasn't even the same. Everything seems so much stranger when you're not here sharing it with me. Now, it ~~was~~ is me leaving you, and for this I couldn't be more sorry. It hurts me so much to know how sad you will be.

I love you winkle, and never forget that no matter what, you will still be able to talk to me, and I will always be able to hear you.

Tell Nathan that I love him and need his forgiveness as well. Be strong for him Erin. He's been through a lot of deaths, and needs your strength.

Please tell DJ that he has been a huge part of my life and I love him so much. Ask him to forgive me for my actions.

A copy of Jessie's original letter, which is considered evidence and is in possession of the Royal Canadian Mounted Police. Under the RCMP stamp across the second page the text reads: " . . . sometimes, Erin. You'll see me in your dreams, and hear my voice in your heart, . . ."

Both Nathan and D.J have ~~been~~ had such a huge impact and made so much difference in my life, They both have always held a special place in my heart. Let them know that.

Tell Clint that I need his forgiveness. Tell him and mom and dad that I love them dearly and I'm sorry. I know Clint is smart and he will make the perfect decission, the best decission for *him* and his future.

Winkalicious you don't know how much I wish that I could have given you one last hug, and snuggle. Just to rub my cheek to yours, and smell you. I miss your smell. God, I prey that you will be alright. I love you more than anything. I love you so much that my heart hurts to think what I will be putting you through. Just remember that this was my choice, and I will be happy. I will be with God and Grandpa. I'll be happy.

Don't forget to talk to me sometimes ████████████████████████████ dreams, and hear my voice in your heart, I'll always be in you, with you, and I'll always listen for you to say my name, and fill me in on the details of your life. I know that this won't be easy to get over, but in time your heart will heal, and you will smile again. Don't give up like I did. Never give up. I love you.

Love your sister-and-best friend. Jessie Jean

CHAPTER NINE

Was That a Sign?

I have changed. With one "enlightenment" after another, I see the world today very differently than I did three years ago. I have always believed in something more than our earthbound existence. I remember sitting around the dining-room table at breakfast some mornings when I was growing up, listening to one of my mother's dreams. It was an event. She rarely remembered her dreams, so when she did it usually meant something. She had an intuition that we all learned to trust and heed. She was downright "spooky."

I realized that I, too, had "spooky" feelings that came true sometimes. I believe we all experience events that we can relate to but have a hard time explaining in rational terms. There is more to us and more to life than this earthly existence. I think we all know it. It's just that, as we have become accustomed to our human, adult ways and our linear thinking, the basic knowledge of who we are gets buried until we can't even imagine anything else. It has taken shattering events in my life to awaken me and help me remember.

Seeing love all around me and feeling it running through me, pumping me full of life, lifting me up and carrying me along in a tide of powerful love energy—that is what started chipping the darkness from my eyes and helping me remember who I am—and who we all are. We are all part of one another. I was ready to see it; I had nothing else. Grief blew me into a state of raw emotion. I didn't care about earthly matters—bills, work. All I could see was how others stepped in to help where they could. My heart was opened up by tragedy, bared to the purity of real love. Everything became different.

I wanted to believe that Jessie was still living in some form, and I understood that she was. You can call this faith, wishful thinking, or the ramblings of a mother unwilling to accept her child's death. Call it what you want, this is my reality. This is real to me and it is the reality of many others like me. Perhaps it is real to you as well. We know Jessie is okay because she has told us in her own way, time and time again. Our love for Jessie has never left us.

This is my understanding: God is Love and God is our Creator; therefore, God, who created us and is the source of all love, created us as little pieces of the whole—part of the love source. Love never ends, and because Jessie was a creation of love, *her* love never ends, either; it can't. We are all part of the same source. But the death of her human form allowed her to go back to that source of love if she chose. I think that perhaps it may be difficult for some to cross over. Just as we become accustomed to our humanness, so we must be acclimatized to our pure state again. This may be especially hard for those not ready to die, or not expecting to. They are jerked from one existence to another and are, for a while, disoriented and lost. Some may not have accepted that they have passed over. Some may not feel they deserve to go to the Love Source yet. Maybe all of our "dearest departed"—even those who were ready to die or chose to die—are bound to us by our grief. They stay close to us as long as we need them. There are signs of this everywhere.

These signs are as individual as each of us is. What is it that we need at that moment? What are we ready for, open to, and willing to see? I saw a little plaque that read, "Bloom where you are planted." But I say that you can bloom even if you are cut.

FALL, 1999—A WAKE-UP CALL FOR JESSIE

E ven in life, we may receive messages to help us open our eyes. They are all around us. Sometimes we practically need to be hit over the head with them before we recognize them. This is what happened to Jessie one day.

She was in a particularly foul mood. She came off as snotty and disrespectful. She dropped by my office (I think her dad had brought her into town from our acreage) to ask for the use of my car. But she snapped and snarled at me. She wanted some money, too, if I recall. It was pretty hard to want to lend her anything when she was acting like that. I told her I didn't appreciate her attitude and that, if she expected me to be giving her anything, she needed to treat me with a little more respect. I said it quite casually, with no preachy tone and no raised voice. I was determined not to let her bad mood put *me* in a bad mood. I had things to do and people to speak to, and it wouldn't do me, or my office any good to be upset.

I gave her the keys and some cash and, as I was explaining when I needed the car again, she snarled some kind of acknowledgement, but no sincere gratitude. I shrugged it off, knowing it was her mood, and I didn't blame her or take offence. An hour or two later, Jessie returned with a smile on her face. Without a word, she gave me a huge hug. She told me she loved me and apologized for being so nasty earlier. She wouldn't tell me what had happened. She sat across from me, waiting for me to finish up what I was doing, a smile lit with wisdom on her peaceful face. Later that day, as we were driving home, Jessie told me what happened that had changed her so.

She had gone to a fast-food establishment in downtown Grande Prairie for salad and fries. As she sat there alone, she noticed a lady and her little daughter sitting at a table not far from her. She thought to herself that the little girl looked a lot like she must have looked when she was that age. The girl had long, dark, wavy hair and big blue eyes. As Jessie watched them, she associated herself with the little girl. She saw her eat and play and squirm in the seat, take off her shoes and brush the hair back from her face. Soon the mother asked the girl to put her shoes back on, as they were about to leave. The little girl didn't want to and started to act up. The more the mom insisted and tried to get the girl to mind, the worse the girl acted until she was in a full-blown temper tantrum, kicking and screaming. The whole restaurant was watching by now and Jessie, still associating, could see the mother's frustration and embarrassment. She started to think about how her antics must have been for me and what I must have gone through. She was just getting the idea when all at once the mother said to the little girl, "Jessie, you put those shoes on right this minute!"

Needless to say, our Jessie got the message loud and clear. It sent shivers through her body. This event, she sensed, was for her benefit—to teach her something. She had already been coming to that understanding, but the little girl sharing the same name with her was like a smack across the face—the final exclamation point.

When she told me that story, I laughed and we talked about what she had learned. I told her the biblical story about Saul and how he had been struck right off his horse before he heard God's message. I told her she had just been knocked off her horse. I think it made her feel a closer relationship with her Creator when she realized that she was worth sending a message to. As I have said before, we all get these messages—sometimes we are just too blind and busy to see, or maybe we don't understand that we all matter enough to have messages sent our way.

OUR BLOSSOM SIGN—JESSIE IS WITH US

Jessie's memorial service was over. We were trying to get back into life again. I had strung the cards we had received—more than four hundred of them—like banners across our ceiling, and I had flowers everywhere around the house. I had created a shrine on our dining room table. Her picture sat in the middle, surround by flower arrangements. A little cherub knelt with its hands cupped on its lap where I placed a yellow ribbon (representing the Yellow Ribbon Light for Life Foundation (see Appendix H). Jessie's New Testament lay open at some verses she had underlined. Her scrapbook was sitting ready to be shared. I had scattered rose petals and hearts around the table and pinned butterfly symbols around her picture frame. On one side of the picture I had placed a bouquet of roses. This was no ordinary bouquet. We had received it as five red roses. Not a half dozen, not one or two, not an even dozen, but five roses. I realized that the person who sent them had intended one rose for each member of our family. One was mine, one Terry's, and there was one for Clint, Erin, and of course Jessie. As the days wore on, flowers in all the arrangements started wilting. I would water and rearrange them to keep them looking nice. But those roses I left alone, just adding water to them from time to time. And, as most roses do, the partly opened buds that we had received turned dark and began to wilt—all but one. It lifted up its head and opened its petals into full bloom. One grey and rainy day as we lay on the couch, feeling especially blue, the sun suddenly broke through the cloud and shone a shaft of light down through our skylight directly upon Jessie's picture, the cherub and the rose. We stood in awe as we marvelled at the ray of light so precise in its focus. Terry grabbed the camera so we could capture this moment for all time.

The rose was a sign, but we were too blinded by grief to see it; however, there was no denying that, just when our hearts were especially low, that ray of light gave us just the message of hope we needed. There was no doubt whatsoever in our minds: Jessie, our flower, was with us. We wept and our hearts were warm in the miracle of it.

The blooming rose, Jessie's picture and the cherub holding a yellow ribbon, momentarily cast in a beam of light from the skylight above, even though it was a cloudy day.

Brittney Kushner had a job picking rocks with a local oilfield service company, tedious and backbreaking work. It was May 24th 2001, a day short of a year since Jessie had died. This was heavy on her mind, and she was feeling the weight of it when all at once she noticed a little butterfly. It hovered and danced, lit and flew all around her on the field as she worked. The same little butterfly stayed close to her as she slaved away in the hot sun. At noon, Brittney sat on the tailgate of the truck to eat her lunch. The butterfly came to the far corner of the tailgate and sat stretching its wings from time to time, but staying right there. Lunch break was over, and Brittney went back to the field. Lo and behold, there it was again. It remained close by her throughout the day. And as she loaded up and drove away, she was sure she saw the little butterfly hovering over the road in the dust she left behind, as if it were saying goodbye. Brittney shared that story with me and asked if I thought it was a sign from Jessie, a message that she was okay and knew that Brittney needed to know that. I told her it wasn't important whether I thought it was a sign. What was important was whether Brittney felt it was. She said she thought so.

"Then," I told her, "if you believe it was a message from Jessie to you, it was."

We didn't know many of Jessie's friend's parents before we lost Jessie, but since, we have become friends. One father also shared a story with me about a butterfly that he recognized as a message from Jessie. It touched this experienced and respected oilfield consultant—who normally never had these kinds of experiences—so deeply that he needed time alone to regroup his thoughts and feelings so he could continue his day.

A lot of people share their butterfly stories with us. They will be thinking of Jessie and missing her when all at once a butterfly will come out of nowhere and fly around them, light on them, light on a shrub or window sill close to them—and just stay there as if it is visiting, bringing joy and peace of mind before it flies on. Brittney found us the little verse that is at the beginning of this book. It says;

A butterfly lights beside us like a sunbeam, and for a brief moment its glory and beauty belong to our world. Then it flies on again, and though we wish it could have stayed, we feel so blessed to have seen it.

                                                                —Unknown.

This little verse seemed so appropriate—as if it were written for Jessie—that we had it engraved on the back of her headstone.

Brittney and Nathan are now married. For a wedding gift, we gave them a large butterfly in a glass frame. They wept.

MOUNTAINS AND RAINBOWS

One day as Terry; Erin; my niece, Jocelyn Lumbama; and I hiked to the summit of Whistler Mountain in Jasper National Park, it began to rain. We were alone on the summit, as other hikers had decided to stop on the trail below us to wait out the showers. We turned to look at the view. My heart was heavy as I began to miss having Jessie with us. This was one of her favourite places on earth. All at once a rainbow spread across the top of the mountain, just out of our reach. Because of our elevation, it was more than a bow; it was almost a circle, its ends stopped only as they met the sides of the mountain. It was so close that it was as if it passed right through us at times, and at the next moment, we felt as though we could reach out and touch it. In all Terry's years and experiences outdoors, he had never witnessed anything like it. I no longer felt the cold or the damp. We all saw it at once and we all stood in wonder at the beauty of it. And without saying a word, we saw in each other's eyes the realization that this was a sign. Jessie was sharing this moment with us.

TERRY'S LITTLE ANGEL

Jessie had a love of horses, too. Don't most people? I know I do. She always wanted one, and we got her one for her birthday one year. The thing was miserable, though, and she never got to ride it. We had to get rid of it before it hurt someone. She used to go and visit horses pastured not far from us. She found comfort in being around them. After we lost her, Terry was having a particularly bad day one time. He was missing Jessie something awful, all the while trying to work. He was standing in line at the bank, blue, stressed, and upset while a little boy full of energy was running around and playing in the line. He was getting on Terry's nerves; Terry wasn't in the mood for this. Once Terry got through the line and was about ready to leave the bank, the little boy ran up to him and said, "I made this for you," then darted out the door with his mom, who was waiting with a smile while her son delivered his gift. Terry had never seen them before, had never spoken to them, and has never seen them since. He looked down at a small piece of paper in his hand. There, drawn in pencil was a small horse with the words, "from Nathan". It made Terry's day a lot brighter. He felt he had been sent a little angel to help him through a rough spot. As I've said before, it always seems that you get just what you need when you need it: a phone call, a song on the radio, a hug from a friend. Whatever it is, it is just the right thing for that moment, and you recognize it as the gift that it is. Thank you, little Nathan, whoever you are, for your special gift.

THE PENNY

Today I found a penny. It's May 15, 2003, ten days before Jessie's Perennial Day. The day has been a busy one, mostly errand-running; but a colleague and I also spoke to a group of Grade 7 and 8 students in Wembley about depression and suicide. In another ten days it will be three years since we lost Jessie. She was hovering in my mind just beyond conscious thought all day. When I spoke to the kids, of course, I was right there, three years ago, holding her in my arms and saying good night, which turned out to be good-bye. I always let myself cry at that point. But then, when the presentation was over, I let her sit back and rest in an easy chair in my mind, just in that quiet little corner where I know she always sits, moving up front from time to time but always in the same room as all my daily thoughts.

Actually, "lost Jessie" is a poor choice of words. We haven't really lost her; she is just not with us in her human form. She was with me today and she let me know it. I had my list: the bank, lunch with Terry, drug store for Terry's prescription, and some dressings and Epsom salts for Clint's injured knee. I'll go to another couple of banks before getting gas and checking the oil and coolant in the car. Then I have to meet the manager of a warehouse store to set up a first-aid drill for tomorrow morning.

I ran through the many little tasks that I had left to do as I filled the gas tank. The wind was blowing like crazy, and I couldn't wait to run inside the little office to pay. The cashier and I discussed the wind and the terrible hailstorm the night before, sharing stories of the stones piled up next to our doors and hoping for a warm sunny day to get our gardening done. As I said good-bye and headed out the door to run for the car, I almost stepped on a bright new penny as I fought the wind for control of the door. I normally would have barely acknowledged it and just kept on with my day. Who has time for a penny? But it had caught the sun and bounced its coppery glow toward my eyes. The instant I saw it, a million thoughts ran through my brain at once. I remembered T. Harv Ecker, entrepreneur and business and personal development trainer, saying how we don't respect money enough and should celebrate finding even a lowly penny. I thought of the phrase we learned to recite at a seminar: "I am a money magnet. Money is attracted to me." I thought of my mom saying the little rhyme "Find a penny, pick it up, and all the day you'll have good luck!" A distant voice, not really audible, still gave me clear direction not to ignore this penny but to take the time to pick it up. "Oh, look," I said, "a penny! I'll have good luck today!"

As the door was closing, whipped from my hand by the wind, the clerk shouted after me: "Put it in your pocket . . . " But I had no pocket to put it in, so I held it in my hand as I drove to my next stop, thinking, "I wonder what year it was minted. What are the chances?" I looked. It was 1982, the year Jessie was born. I burst into tears. I knew that I was not alone; Jessie was with me. I didn't see her or hear her voice; I didn't need to. She spoke to me loud and clear through a little copper penny.

It was November 1, 2001. Terry had to run into town on business and I was alone in the house. I was feeling frustrated because Terry and our guests from Penticton, B.C., who were taking a tour of the countryside, had received some experiences of messages from "the other side" over the last few days, and I was a little jealous. I didn't understand why I couldn't. I believed that I could. Perhaps I was trying too hard. I just needed to relax and let it happen in its own time. I was doing dishes and not thinking of anything in particular. I took the cutlery out of the rinse sink, placing these utensils in the drying rack. I sorted the knives, forks, and spoons into separate spots and then changed my mind. I wanted to switch the spoons and the forks. All at once Jessie was teasing me. It wasn't that I heard words spoken aloud; it was more like a sensation of words in my mind—but they were *hers*. She was making fun of me for making such a big deal out of where I placed the cutlery to dry. It was like, "And you thought *I* was bad!"

This referred to how I teased her when we went shopping. I would put things in the cart and she would cast me a dirty look, shake her head and rearrange the goods neatly in the cart. I teased her about that every time she did it. It became a game. And there she was, her words as clear in my mind as if she had spoken them in my ear. I was stopped in mid-motion and I clutched my chest. I staggered back a few steps and began to laugh out loud. She caught me red-handed, doing exactly what I used to tease her about. Then I cried. But these were tears of joy, for it was in that instant that I realized that Jessie had not left me. Only our relationship and the way we communicate had changed. I had shared a new moment with the daughter I thought I had lost. I have not had another experience like that, but I don't need one. That experience of November 1, 2001, is all I needed. It was so real and clear to me that it cast away any lingering doubts that may have been lurking in the dark corners of my mind. I have not lost her; she is always with me. The pain of missing her scent, her touch, the feel of her skin, her hair, to see her eyes and hear her laughter—that pain I carry with me. But there is comfort in knowing that her love is with me in whatever I do, and she is with me when I need her most.

DREAM VISITS FOR WINKIE (ERIN)

Erin was upset one day when we were talking about signs. Why couldn't she ever have a clear sign? When she sees a butterfly, it is just a butterfly. Nothing ever happened to touch her and her alone. No real feeling that Jessie was right there with *her*. I asked her, "You dream of Jessie don't you?" She told me she did. I asked how often. Every night that she remembered her dreams, Jessie had been in them. And it wasn't as if she was dreaming about Jessie, it was just that whatever was going on in the dream, Jessie was there with Erin, sharing in it. She knew in her dream that Jessie was dead, but Jessie was there anyway. I told Erin that I had not once had a Jessie dream. Not once. I reminded her that Jessie told her that she would always be there for her Winkie Doodle Bug. She would never leave her; Erin would see her in her dreams. I told Erin that I believed that she wasn't just dreaming of Jessie; Jessie was visiting her in the dreams.

"She is by you each and every night. She will always be with you. She lives with you, shares experiences with you, and travels with you, all in your dreams." Now Erin will tell me, "Jessie and I went skidooing last night. It was so much fun!" Or she will tell how they danced all night and won a dance contest, or other things that they do together in her dreams. Jessie kept her promise.

LOOKING AFTER MAMMA

The road to Hinton was a journey I thought I was taking alone. I was wrong.

Hinton is about a four-hour drive from Grande Prairie following Highway 40 to Grande Cache, then on until the junction with another highway. Hang a right and you are only a short drive to Jasper National Park and the beautiful mountain town of Jasper. Head left at the junction instead, and you find yourself in the forestry town of Hinton. Well travelled by transport trucks and the odd soul like me, this mountain highway has little in the way of civilized amenities, but the splendour of nature greets you at almost every turn. Wildlife is plentiful—deer, elk and moose—and although there are signs of human activities in the oil and gas industry, forestry, and coal mining, most of what meets your eye is the foothills and valleys that blend into the Rocky Mountains.

It was a beautiful day to travel, very warm for March in northern Alberta. The sun was shining through my windshield, warming me as I drove. I had tunes playing on the radio and I sang along, smiling to myself. The road was free of ice, snow, and heavy traffic. The car, which my husband feared was becoming unreliable, was running as smoothly as a cheetah on the Serengeti. I was content.

I had been asked to examine students who had just finished a two-week course qualifying them as Advanced First Aiders and preparing them to register as Emergency Medical Responders. I was looking forward to tomorrow; I like meeting new people, and being with them when they achieve a crucial step in their lives. I was also looking forward to getting to the motel in Hinton this evening where I could just kick back and vegetate. I had brought a book to read and was anxious to get started on it. No interruptions, no one needing me to do something for them, no phone calls, just "me" time.

Then it happened: clanging and grinding and clattering coming from my engine. The tachometer showed the engine's revolutions per minute (rpm)—it was turning over all right, but there was no power. My mileage counter showed I was still about fifty kilometres from Grande Cache. I glanced at my cell phone but there was no cell service. I knew by the sound of it that my motor was pretty much gone anyway, and I felt I didn't have much choice but to push it as far at it would take me. This is unsettling, for as soon as one hears noises like that in an engine, the natural reflex is to get off the road quickly and shut it down. But these were not normal circumstances. I was a woman travelling alone on a mountain highway. Where I was, it wasn't safe to stop. There are no real shoulders to speak of, and few roadside pullout areas. Once I did find a place to pull over, my only option was going to be a fifty-kilometre hike. I decided to trim that distance down. I didn't want to be walking in the dark. I pushed my Chrysler Intrepid hard, coasting it down hills like a soapbox cart and coaxing it up hills with sweet talk, "Come on, baby, you can do it." But it couldn't, and finally it stopped running altogether. I rolled to a stop in a valley, pulled as far off the driving lane as possible, and turned on my flashers. I was twenty-three kilometres from Grande Cache.

I could walk that. There was some good daylight left, I had my winter emergency pack with me, and I had packed snacks and water for the trip. I wasn't scared, worried, or even concerned. It was as though I knew everything would be okay, and it was all very matter-of-fact. I sat for a minute planning my next move. A few trucks had passed me going both directions, without so much as slowing down. I changed into a warmer jacket, grabbed mitts and a toque, and was gathering up some trail mix, matches, tea bags, water and such. I know enough about the mountains to know how fickle the weather can be. One moment Mother Nature is smiling warmly on your face and the next minute she's throwing a snowy tantrum. I knew I had to be prepared. I had to think about personal safety, too. I decided to walk facing oncoming traffic so I could see vehicles coming, but also so that if someone did stop, I could run in the direction opposite to the way the vehicle was facing if their intentions were to hurt rather than help. If someone stopped going the same direction as I, there would be the width of the road between us.

I thought to myself, "How sad it is that I need to think this way. I wish I didn't have to think of the ill nature of a few people in this world." I decided to focus on the goodness in it. I was just about ready to start my trek when a couple pulled over in a half-ton truck and asked if I needed help.

"Actually", I said, "I would appreciate if you could send a tow truck for me from Grande Cache."

"And leave you here on the side of the road? We can't do that. We can give you a ride to town. You aren't safe out here on the highway. Do you know how many crazy people there are?"

I gratefully accepted the offer, grabbed my bags and jumped in with them. I learned that they were on an impromptu holiday. They were from north of Manning, Alberta, and were just following their noses to see where they'd end up. They thought they might eventually find themselves in the Okanogan Valley, visiting family there.

They drove me to a gas station where it seemed there might be a tow truck service. My newfound friends asked if I had an AMA (Alberta

Motor Association) card. I had let mine lapse and hadn't got around to renewing it. We discovered that the tow truck that took AMA was in Edmonton and wouldn't be back until ten that night. It wasn't even five o'clock yet. We sat in the vehicle and discussed our next move. We hadn't even introduced ourselves yet.

"My name is Faris Atkinson, by the way," I said as I extended a hand from the back seat. They laughed.

"Atkinson? You won't believe this, but our names are Atkinson, too!" We found out we knew some of the same people, but we had never heard of each other before this. I used my cell and called Terry. We discussed our options. The Atkinsons decided that they would use their AMA card and have my car towed for me all the way back to Grande Prairie. Then they insisted on driving me to Hinton and ensuring I was safe in my motel. On the way, I phoned Erin.

"Hi, baby bear! It's Momma. I just wanted to let you know where I am and what's up." I told her the story and of these wonderfully generous people. She told me to be sure to say hello to them for her and to thank them for looking after me. I did so.

"You have a daughter named Erin?" Mrs. Atkinson asked, "So do we!"

A few hours later, as I sat alone in my motel room, I took a minute and thanked my angels for watching over me. With all those little "signs" I knew I was to get the message that I had long before figured out: I am never alone, and the Atkinsons were heaven-sent.

WE GET WHAT WE NEED

W e get what we need when we need it in a way that we can relate to it and understand it, in a way that won't frighten us but will do what it is intended to do—comfort us.

These are but a few of the experiences that we have lived. There are many more. How can we think that there is nothing more to life than this physical existence? I don't believe Jessie creates the rainbow or makes the rose bloom or is the butterfly. But experiencing these things connects our spirits. The experiences are a catalyst linking us across space and time, and I am glad that I am able to recognize them for what they are—gifts of love, from love, the force that binds us together and can never be broken.

OUR NEWEST TRADITION

Has an idea ever come to you in the early hours of the morning, just before you are fully awake? It seems so clear and makes so much sense that you wonder why you never thought of it before. It is almost as if it is coming from someone else as they speak to you in your sleep. You are still sleepy and you think that you'll never forget this idea because it is just too good; you'll write it down when you get up. Sometimes falling back to sleep and getting up later has diminished the clarity of that wondrous image, and sometimes you forget it altogether. Early one December morning in 2003, an idea came to me as if it was being whispered in my ear. As I lay there thinking that I should get up to write this down, and on the verge of convincing myself that I would do it later when I was fully awake, the voice in my head got louder and louder until I found myself sitting on the edge of my bed and reaching for my sweater and socks.

The idea was powerful and clear; I picked up a pen and note pad and began to write. The words flowed from the pen, and I could envision everything as it would unfold. I would like to say that this was my idea, but I cannot; it came from several places. I am just the mixing pot, the instrument.

Think of the possibilities. This same idea of combining rituals or traditions to make a new one can be applied to anyone and any event, not just those of us who celebrate Christmas!

For us, though, this would be a new Christmas tradition; a combination of the lighting of Advent candles and the candle lighting service that Oliver's Funeral Chapel holds every year as described in the Introduction. I could imagine the Atkinson family gathering at the home in Hythe of Terry's sister and brother-in-law, Lorraine and Cliff Rule. Their son Dillon would be there. He works in Australia and wasn't home for Christmas 2002. This was especially hard on him and his family, but we all missed him. He decided that he would not spend another Christmas alone in Australia and flew home to be with us. Patsy's girl, Caroline, was going to be in Disneyland with her husband, Fabian (Fab), their three-year-old son, Keegan, and Fab's family on Christmas day, so they wouldn't be with us this year. We all would be thinking of those we missed, both living and passed on, and the idea was that we would actually have some kind of commemoration acknowledging that.

I knew most of Terry's family would have no clue about what Advent was, let alone the Advent wreath and traditions behind it. After writing down the idea that came in my half-awake – half-asleep state, I called Terry's sister Lorraine to see if it was something she thought the family would like to do. She loved it. We started to plan the logistics. I did some research on Advent wreaths and fleshed out the little "service" we would do just before our Christmas meal. I wrote and memorized a script, complete with stage directions, using some of the words from the Oliver's Candle Lighting Service. And I created a wreath.

The Atkinson family tradition is that we go to one of our homes for Christmas dinner each year. Last year, Caroline and Fab had us to their new home. Christmas 2004 would be at our place.

On Christmas Day, 2003, I placed an Advent wreath as a centrepiece on the table as we were all gathering at the Rule house. There were lots of questions, but I said we were doing something a bit different this year and it would be explained later. Finally dinner was ready. We gathered everyone around the table. There are too many to sit at one table, so we usually eat buffet style. Everyone stood and circled the table as I began to speak the words I had written.

You are all wondering about this wreath on our table this year. This is what I hope to be the start of a new family tradition. It is called an Advent wreath, but it will be much more than that for us. Let me explain.

When I was growing up, we knew all about Advent. Our church had a wreath and, on the fourth Sunday before Christmas, a candle was lit. Then on the next Sunday, that first candle was lit as well as a second candle. The third Sunday, three candles were lit and so on. Most churches do a similar thing every Christmas season. We also had a wreath at home and we would have a little family candle-lighting service.

Advent means "coming" or "arrival". The spirit of Advent is expectation, anticipation, preparation, and a longing or yearning for peace. Each part of the wreath is symbolic. Some of the symbols date back even before Christianity. The Celts used wreaths with candles lit during the cold, dark December days as a sign of hope for the future warm, bright days of spring. In Scandinavia, lighted candles were placed on a wheel, and prayers were offered to the god of light to turn the wheel of earth back toward the sun to lengthen the days and restore warmth.

The wreath is made of evergreen: pine, holly and yew stand for immortality, cedar for strength and healing. Cones, seedpods or nuts symbolize faith and resurrection. The circle of the wreath stands for everlasting life, the fact that love has no beginning or end. Altogether, the wreath represents the immortality of our soul and the promise of new and everlasting life.

The Candles stand for the light of love in the world and the darkness of fear and hopelessness receding each week as more light radiates into the world. Jesus said, "I am the light of the world." Each of us is a creation of light. The candles celebrate that and allow us to see things more clearly and feel warmth.

The colours mean something, too. Purple or violet was the colour of royalty, welcoming the advent of a King. Purple also signifies suffering and is used during Lent and through Easter. This points to an important connection between Jesus' birth and death. The colour rose holds its meaning in the Catholic tradition in which the Pope gives his Cardinals roses on the fourth Sunday of Lent; that colour then found its way into the fourth Sunday of Advent. It was meant to bring joy and brightness into the waiting.

The lighting of the Advent candles is in preparation for the coming of Christ and the promise of peace he was to bring the world. Each candle represents a step in the journey to Christmas.

Candle 1 (purple) stands for hope or expectation and is commonly associated with the prophets as they foretold the coming of the Messiah.

Candle 2 (purple) stands for peace, for John the Baptist who prepared the world for Jesus' message of peace, or for Bethlehem.

Candle 3 (purple) stands for love, shepherds, or the Magi and reminds us of dedication, admiration, and love for the Christ Child.

Candle 4 (pink) stands for Christmas joy, Mary, or angels, and for joyful hearts and joyful voices.

The centre candle is white, representing purity and truth. It is usually called the Christ Candle and stands for Christ, the light of the world (some advent wreaths do not have the centre candle).

The last, centre candle is lit on Christmas Day. The Prince of Peace has come. Peace on earth! But where is the peace? People are still at war; they still do horrible things to each other every day. God knows the atrocities that humanity has inflicted on humanity under the banner of Christianity. But I now understand the peace that Jesus brought. It was the peace of understanding that this life is not all there is. The essence of who we are, our soul or spirit, our love light, that is our true self and it will never die. That is what Jesus brought the world: a promise of life everlasting and peace in our hearts when we lose someone we love. Now we know that they are not gone forever.

The Christmas story tells of angels on high talking to shepherds and filling the skies with singing. It speaks of wise men following a star in the heavens. These stories help us understand that heaven and earth are closer than we think. They are intertwined; they exist together. The two worlds—the physical and the spiritual—are not at all separate. That is what the Christmas story is telling us.

Today I want to start a new family tradition.

The Advent wreath has new meaning for me now. Today, instead of lighting the four candles on the outside first, I light the centre candle. This candle represents to me not only a promise of life after death and of love that has no beginning or end; it also symbolizes all those whom we have loved, whom we continue to love, but who are with us only in spirit. It will also be for those who are alive but can't be with us physically today. With our family growing, building families of their own, travelling and working far from home, we won't have the opportunity to come together at Christmas as we used to. I wanted to do this now, at Christmas, because each year, someone is missing from the table. We think of them. They are always with us and it feels good to acknowledge them somehow. I chose to use a traditional wreath so that no matter where we are in the world, whenever we see an Advent wreath, we will feel our family with us.

From the centre candle we light the others, and I'll ask various people around the table to do the honours.

Candle 1: "For all of those who journeyed with us in a special way, those who shared with us during our youth and adulthood and who enriched our family life, this candle is lit for our brothers and sisters, aunts and uncles, cousins, nieces, nephews and friends. Cliff, would you light this for us?" *(Any of us could have lit this candle, but I asked Cliff as he lost a brother years ago and I knew he still grieves for him every day).*

Candle 2 : "This candle is lit for those who gave us life and nurtured us, our mothers and fathers, grandparents, and in-laws. Patsy, would you light this one?" *(I thought it fair that Patsy, the oldest of the Atkinson siblings, light the candle in memory of her dad, Allan. I had considered Jackie, too, as she had lost her father when she was very young, but I tried to have a member of each family take part and I had plans for Jackie and Roy's oldest daughter, Jennifer, to light a candle later).*

Candle 3: "This candle is lit for those whose love enriched us in a special way: our wives, husbands, fiancées, or life partners. Granny or Willy?" *(Both had lost spouses, so I wanted to let them choose who would light the candle. Granny Vi did.)*

Candle 4 : "For those we were privileged to give life to: our sons and daughters, grandchildren and babies lost before they were born. Jennifer, I'd like you to light this one." *(Jennifer had had a miscarriage about four years earlier. I knew how much it hurt her and how she grieved the loss of a baby she would never know. I think we tend to forget that a miscarriage can be a devastating loss, and I wanted her to know we remembered and cared.)*

Lorraine bought taper candles for each of us and had passed them out so we all had our own candle to hold. I said:

Now we light our own taper candles off one of the wreath candles and think of those people we miss the most right now, quietly and privately.

Some people lit off more than one candle. I noticed Granny touched her candle to every one in the wreath.

I nodded to Erin and Jasmine, who had been asked to start the CD player on queue. "I'll be home for Christmas" played while we held our flickering candles.

After the song was done, I said:

Christmas is about uniting family and being together again. These candles burning at our tables each Christmas are a reminder that we are all together again, here and now, complete in the love we have for each other. This is something we can be thankful for and celebrate. Every Christmas we can look at the candles and we will see the glow and feel warmth and peace in our hearts because we are complete as a family.

When ready, extinguish your candle. Take your time. It's just a safety issue: Twenty or so candles burning all over the house isn't a great idea.

That is how it went. Many tears were shed and I was thanked over and over for leading us in that little service. For most it was a mix of joy and pain: joy in acknowledging those we miss most, and pain in missing them. For some it brought recognition that, although we share a lot of pain as a family, we each have our own individual wounds as well. Probably the best comment came from someone grieving who told me of a new understanding—that a lost loved one is not really gone but has a living spirit that remains with us. The person had heard this many times before, but had just now really come to understand and believe it. "Thank you for giving me Christmas back," this person said.

I was at peace for the whole 2003 Christmas season for the first time in years. Terry told me that he was, too. We didn't do this for ourselves as much as for the family. After being thanked for giving someone their Christmas back, I said a silent "Thank You" to whoever guided me to the idea of the wreath and candle-lighting, and I realized how blessed I was to recognize the power of a simple ceremony. I was also grateful to Lorraine and the rest of the family for being open enough to participate. I am moved and awed each time I think of it.

I am including this for you to take and use. You don't have to have a Christian background to follow the same idea. Alter it as best fits your family, beliefs, or circle of friends, and use it if it will help you to heal.

CHAPTER TEN

What Is It
About a Butterfly?

S ince Jessie died, butterflies have become a significant symbol, not just for our family and me, but for many others as well. You read some butterfly stories in chapter nine, and I wanted to share with you why it means so much to us, and what butterflies have meant to other cultures and religions.

Jessie loved butterflies; they were one of her favourite things. She loved rainbows (a symbol of promise, hope and life), and daisies. She also liked roses. She received a great many and she dried them all and saved them. She had them hanging on string, single roses all across her bedroom ceiling; it was raining roses in her room. Jessie loved nature and was especially fond of the mountains. We live close to the Rockies, and spending time in those mountains remains a favourite pastime. I still get weepy going to the mountains without her. And while I am there, I feel her presence with me at every turn. For some reason, though, we have found ourselves connecting butterflies especially with Jessie. We have grown to feel that sometimes a butterfly is just a butterfly, and at other times it is a message from Jessie. The difference is the feeling we get when we are near it, or watching it.

Have you ever really thought about butterflies? They start out as tiny eggs sticking to the underside of a little leaf. They enter the world as a minuscule, worm-like being with lots of tiny legs. Their whole universe is that tiny leaf. All they know is what they need, and all they need is to eat leaf and hide from anything that might want to gobble them up. They are earthbound and narrow-minded. Even as they eat and grow, and their world expands, they still believe the plant they are on is the universe. That's all there is. Oh, they might wonder if there is something more to the world, something more to life, but they don't know for sure and so it can't be real. Quick! Roll into a ball! Tuck your tail and head in! Hide! Something nasty is trying to devour you! Then soon it is time for this life to draw to a close. Little caterpillar builds her cocoon. She has worked all her life, focused on surviving, eating and dodging an early demise. For what? To die anyway? To lie inside the coffin she builds herself? What a life. But wait! There's more! That may be the end of life as she knew it, life in her familiar earthbound form. Yes, the caterpillar is dead, but the butterfly that was her true self, never died. Out of the coffin emerges a new creature with a slender body and bright wings, not destined to stay attached to this plant, but able to ride the wind. This plant was only such a tiny little piece of the universe. She now sees there is much more, beyond her wildest imagination, and it seems endless. Her purpose now is to live and bring new life to the world, to keep the cycle going, to fly, to sip nectar, to love, and to create. No wonder the butterfly means so much to so many. She represents resurrection, new life, freedom, and spirit.

BUTTERFLY SYMBOLISM

Butterflies are a symbol of many things to many different people, cultures and generations. They represent change, and when they fly they look as though they are drifting and floating on the breeze to the rhythm of our hearts. They inspire us to let go of what weighs us down, to take the time to light on a flower and appreciate its offerings, to dance on the wind and be free.

According to a First Nations legend, if you have a secret wish, you should capture a butterfly and whisper your secret to it. A butterfly can't speak, so your secret is safe with it. When you release the butterfly, your wish is carried to the Great Spirit, who alone knows the thoughts of butterflies. Because you set the butterfly free, you are helping to restore the balance of nature, so your wish will be granted.

In many religions, including Christianity, the butterfly is a symbol of transformation and rebirth. In early Christianity, it represented a soul. Today the butterfly is still used as a symbol of life after death—metamorphosis.

It is a symbol often associated with Easter because of the similar transformation of Jesus at his resurrection.

The butterfly leaves the safety of its cocoon and greets a brand new world as a whole different being. This can be a powerful image to motivate someone to seek change in their life, not to be afraid of change, or to inspire change around them. All require courage.

It is interesting to learn that the word "psyche" is Greek for both "soul" and "butterfly". In ancient Greece, it was believed that butterflies were actually human souls flying about looking for a new incarnation.

You've heard about the birds and the bees? The Celts thought pregnancy occurred when a woman swallowed a butterfly soul, and the butterfly souls flew around looking for a new mother to take them in! In one culture, it is believed that the butterfly's soul can leave the body in sleep, and that accounts for dreams. I know it does for Erin's dreams! Our Jessie butterfly flies to her almost every night, as discussed in chapter nine.

One of our young friends who knew Jessie, Jordan Walega, created a unique and beautiful butterfly. Its body is almost feminine in its shape. In an allusion to motion, it has images of feathers and ribbons. I can get lost in it as my eyes follow its lines. A ghost image overlaps the butterfly form, and subtle waves seem to radiate from it.

Butterflies have always been noticed, admired, and wondered upon, but to us—Jessie's friends and family—they remind us of our Jessie and her love transformed into an angel with blue eyes, dark wavy hair and angel wings as colourful as flower petals.

CHAPTER ELEVEN

Helping Someone
Who's Grieving

I realize that this book may be read by people who have not suffered traumatic loss themselves but who wish to understand those who have. My stories, shared with you, may already have given you a good idea of how to help someone. This chapter will summarise some of those ideas and perhaps provide a few other helpful thoughts.

Talking and listening: Most people want to talk about the one they have lost. They want to share their thoughts, maybe even their feelings, but mostly, they are holding on to their loved one through memories, and memories are best saved when shared with someone else. Allow the bereaved to talk. All you need do is listen. They may ask "Why?" but you don't need all the answers. Often, we really don't expect one; we are just trying to understand what has happened and find some rationale for the pain. All you need do is say you don't know why and continue to listen. Don't minimize what they feel. If it is important enough for them to share with you, then it is important to acknowledge as a part of their grief.

I remember teaching a first aid class one day when one of my students received a phone call. It was important enough to interrupt the class. The staff had taken the call and informed me that this girl might be about to receive some bad news, and perhaps I'd better stand by to support her if she needed it. By her reactions and expressions as she listened to the person on the other end of the phone, I could tell she was devastated by what she heard. I recognized it—the disbelief, the excruciating pain. She crumpled into my arms and wept openly. I gave her some tissue and tried to console her. I tried to imagine what she had been told. I assumed that someone she loved had died, but I had no idea who. She wasn't able to tell me for a while. Finally she apologized for carrying on as she had. I told her that an apology wasn't necessary. She explained that it was necessary, and she was embarrassed for acting as she had.

Her mom had been on the phone. This young girl had just learned her pet cat had died. I could have laughed at her, belittled her, and told her that she was right; she didn't have a reason for carrying on that way for a cat. But I knew better. This was probably the first real loss this girl had ever had in her life. That cat obviously meant the world to her. Grief is grief, pain is pain, and it is not up to me to tell anyone how she should feel or think. Just because I have lost parents and a daughter, do I have the right to say I really understand what grief is, and she doesn't have a right to grieve as I did? No. It is for me to acknowledge her pain and help her through it if she needs me to. I'm glad I was there for her, and I hope that if and when she loses a parent, child, friend, cousin or whomever, that someone will be there to help her through. Remember that sometimes no words are necessary. All you need to do is hold the bereaved and let them know you care.

Anytime is a good time: Maybe two or three weeks after a loss, call or drop by. Everything has quietened down. Folks have gone back to routine. But the bereaved are all at once alone with their feelings and trying to get through daily living with all the stressors that are involved in that. Sometimes, you may have been thinking that you should call, or send a card, or drop by, but as time goes on, you get feeling more awkward about it. Soon it may be months, and you have yet to speak to them for the first time after their loss. The more time that passes, the harder it gets.

I'll let you in on something: There is so much going on around you when you first lose someone and you are living in a daze that you don't even notice if a certain friend is missing or hasn't called. You are so overwhelmed by it all, and so many well-wishers surround you, that you know everyone who cares about you is with you in spirit, if not in person. Remember that you get what you need when you need it. At a social function recently, we ran into some people who had been our neighbours years ago. The man was so upset that he hadn't spoken to us since we lost Jessie more than two years earlier that he was embarrassed and overly apologetic. He felt as though he had let us down, and he was carrying tremendous guilt about not being there for us. What he needed to know was that his timing was perfect. We needed to connect with him at this time; we needed to be able to share what we had already shared with so many. We needed to share this with fresh ears and an open heart willing to hear it. Don't be afraid to call someone who lost a loved one, say, five years ago, and say, "I was thinking of you. How are you? It's been a long time and I feel like I wasn't there for you then, but I'm here now." You have no idea how wonderful it is to know that, even though so much time has passed, someone acknowledges the continuing pain of your loss.

"If there is anything I can do . . .": How many times have you heard that? You may have heard those words coming from your own lips; I know I have. Those words are always comforting to hear. But when we are in pain, and still even a bit in shock and disbelief, we aren't going to ask you for anything. Often we can't think of anything at such a time. The things I remember most are those special people who have the gift of just doing. This is an area that I still need to work at, but it seems to come naturally to others. They take it upon themselves, unasked, to help care for small children, do laundry, polish shoes—any number of things.

One day I was at my office in town. A paramedic friend of mine who hadn't been by my office before, showed up with his partner. It was getting close to Christmas 2000. Mitch Walker walked right in and, without saying a word, just gave me a huge hug. He uttered a few words, letting me know that my family and I were in his and his family's prayers. Mitch said a very few words that I don't even recall while his partner stood by the door in silence. Then, Mitch turned and left. As his partner went to follow him I said, "So do you just follow him around all day while he delivers hugs?" "Pretty much," was the reply—and just like that they were gone. We aren't really close friends,

Mitch and I, but we are always glad to see each other and exchange greetings in passing, and most often we hug. But that day, he was a gift from God. Like an angel, he floated into my life for that brief moment and gave me exactly what I needed. No more and no less. That few minutes he took out of his busy day to give me a hug helped me get through that whole day and then some. Even now as I remember it, I feel blessed to have special people like him in my life. You never know how much a simple act will mean to someone. I still feel a glow in my heart when I picture Dawn Calvert making butterfly corsages for Jessie's memorial, Georgina Roche as she bounced along over our four-acre yard on her ride on mower, my sisters decorating the hall where the service was going to be held, the food donated and prepared by loving hands, the housework done, the repairs made, the visits—on and on it goes, and it continues yet! A phone call may be just a phone call to you, but to the one who receives it, it can feel heaven-sent. We are all instruments of God. We just don't realize it most of the time. Don't be afraid to do even the simplest act of love for someone. It is remembered and appreciated long after it is done, and the love energy from that act is renewed, and new strength gained each time it is remembered.

Health-care professionals, councillors, and clergy grieve, too: These people are always there for us when we suffer loss. They give us professional guidance and help as we learn to cope. What if it is they who are the bereaved? Too often, we feel that they know how to deal with this. We think to ourselves, "What have I got to offer them to help them through their grief?" The truth is that they need our support just as much as the rest of us do, maybe more. As they are themselves trying to cope with loss, they may have to help others through losses, too. I have spoken to several professionals who have suffered in silence, not able to share their grief because no one offered to listen. Where can they go? If you are their friend, let them know you are there for them to talk to. Start the topic and then listen. What you can offer them—an open heart, open arms and listening ears—is "just what the doctor ordered."

Available Resources: Most communities have resources that should be mentioned to the grieving as options to help them through the pain, Doctors and clergy are but two. There may be grief counsellors, support groups, help lines, mental-health support, victim's assistance, walk-in clinics, and a whole variety of other choices to assist people struggling through the anguish. As a friend, you can offer to find help, set appointments, go with them—whatever they wish. You don't need to give advice; you just need to be a friend who cares, listens, and can offer a few small acts of kindness. One of those acts may be suggesting resources in your community or a community near you that you know about. You can mention them to your bereaved friend when he or she seems lost and you feel you have done all you can. It may take time after the loss before they are ready to talk to a "stranger" about how they feel, so you may not want to mention it *immediately* after the loss. But the sooner they can receive some special TLC from folks trained and experienced in that kind of care, the more they can benefit by it.

Love is the strongest healer. If you are sincere in whatever you can offer, those who grieve can feel it and will be grateful for every kind word, thought and prayer.

We are the architects of our own lives. The foundation, framework, and supports of our lives are our friends, family, support groups, and other resources in our communities. We build our lives out of many things, but the structure first needs to be sound. It is all held together with acts of love. This is the concrete, nails, glue, caulking and mortar, without which nothing would hold together. But we are in control of our lives; we make the choices. We need to accept the mortar given us and use it well. If we don't construct a solid foundation, if we neglect the effort of careful planning and proper maintenance, the next storm will knock us down. If the earth shakes beneath us, our lives will come crashing down in rubble around us. But the building blocks are all still there. And if we took care and attended to those blocks all this time, they will be there for us to use once more. They haven't fallen far from where we need them to start building again. The acts of love will be new and fresh, ready to hold us together again. All we need do is recognize and accept them. Putting our lives back together after we crumble is slow and painful work, but we are never doing it alone as long as we have tended to our lives, our friends, and our family with love and care when they were chipped and broken.

Those who grieve need closure, something to help them know that the cause of their grief is real and to help them come to terms with it. For many there are a number of steps to this closure: it doesn't happen with just one event. Some people feel they must be with the departed loved one's body, to touch it, kiss it, say good-bye. I don't need that. As a matter of fact, I feel quite traumatized by open-casket funerals and I won't approach or look at the body. I need to remember a person as she was alive, not as a shell. The person I remember does not live in that body any more.

But just because I don't like it doesn't make it wrong; it is only wrong for me. Remember that: If someone doesn't want to see their loved one's body to say good-bye, don't make them. There are other ways to find closure: the service, an interment, a scattering-of-the-ashes ceremony, a wake, the continuing sharing of memories—all these can help bring closure.

I had to tell my uncle, my father's only brother and oldest sibling, that he couldn't view his baby brother's body. I did that because I knew my parent's wishes. They had told me that when they passed away, they wanted to be cremated before any memorial service. They had that wish written in their will. They said they didn't want anyone to see their dead bodies. So I upheld their wish and, though I'm glad I did, I realize now how hard it was for my wonderful Uncle Louis Swallow. He really needed to see Dad. I know that now, and it hurts sometimes when I think of it because now he's gone and I can't tell him that I understand and I'm truly sorry.

When my sweet grandmother, Helen Jean Lee, passed away in November 2002, in New Westminster, B.C., my sister Marilyn told me she wanted to "prepare" her body. I wasn't sure what she meant by that. My sister Heather accompanied her with some anxiety, as she, too, was unsure what this "preparing" was going to entail. When I finally arrived from Grande Prairie (Terry, Erin, and I drove the thirteen-hour trip to Vancouver), Heather told me of her adventure with our youngest sister. They went to the funeral home together. They entered a brightly lit room where our grandmother lay draped with a linen sheet on a cold metal table in the centre of this environment of white and stainless steel.

Marilyn asked Heather if she remembered to bring the dress that Grandma was going to be buried in. Heather, wide-eyed and hesitant, said she didn't have it and hurriedly offered to drive over to pick it up. She felt a sense of relief in being able to escape that place for even a little while.

Upon her return, however, she found a much different atmosphere. The lights were dim, there were candles burning, and there was soft music playing. Marilyn had just finished washing Grandma's hair. Heather felt peace overcome her anxiety, and she began to help in the ritual. They washed Grandma lovingly with scented water, and massaged her with fragrant oils. They dressed her in her best dress, stockings, and shoes, and put on the new sweater she had just received as a birthday gift. They fixed her hair and covered her with a beautiful afghan. Before they left, each said good-bye in her own way. Heather felt that Grandma would have been pleased with it all. I am glad that Marilyn did that, and I am happy that Heather took part. It is a beautiful memory of a loving act, not just for Grandma, but also for those of us who couldn't or wouldn't participate, and Marilyn and Heather share it as sisters. I feel good knowing it was they who got her body ready for its final rest. And I think it was the perfect closure for Heather. She was very close to Gran, as she spent the most time with her and looked after her affairs over the last few years of her life. It was she who would probably miss Grandma the most. I am proud of her courage in taking that opportunity, which our amazing, free-spirited sister, Marilyn, envisioned.

My closure came in the service, which I prepared and led. I found therapy in doing it and was happy I could do something for Grandma, her friends, and our family. Our other sister, Lee Ann, brought her guitar,

Clinton and Helen Jean (Grandma) Lee, 1998. Clint is 18 and Gran is 88.

and singing together as one family was another special moment and gift to one another. Grandma belonged to the United Church next door to the funeral chapel, but we had the service in the funeral chapel so that our brother Curtis, a Jehovah's Witness, could attend. We were thinking of one another with love.

I remember driving to the service at the funeral chapel. I was still scribbling a few things, trying to get everything organized. Terry was driving, Erin was in the back seat of the truck, and I had my papers spread across my lap. All at once, as I was reading what I had just written, I heard my Grandmother speak to me. "What's all this fuss about?" I heard her say. "You don't need to be doing all this balderdash!"

I laughed out loud. At the same instant, Terry asked me what the smell was. I said, "What smell?" He said it was like an old-person smell. Erin said she smelled it, too. We had met with our brother-in-law, Chris Lumbama, and his daughter, Jocelyn, and given hugs, and I could still smell Chris's lingering scent of cologne on me. Maybe that is what they smell. No, it wasn't that, they said; it was more like flowery, powdery perfume. I couldn't smell what they smelled, but I shared with them what I had just experienced, Gran's comment to me. We all sat quietly smiling and basked in the moment. Grandma was right there with us. What a wonderful gift!

The point is that over and over we have found strength and support in giving and receiving acts of love. We pull together as a family; we put aside any differences we might have. We think of each other first, and in that we find closure, comfort, and some peace.

Giving to others is actually a selfish thing. I find such joy in the giving that I feel as if I did it for myself!

Sometimes giving is easier than receiving, but I have learned to take the gifts I'm given with gratitude because I realize that the person I am getting them from has just felt better in the giving of it.

It is the acts of love and the people who give them that are the source of our strength. It has been the source of my strength, and my inspiration to carry on.

Love is the only truth.
It is only in the sharing of Love that it grows, blossoms and flies on
Flower-petal wings from heart to heart and bloom to bloom.

Handling the Holidays

A PRESENTATION FOR THE
OLIVER'S FUNERAL CHAPEL AND CREMATORIUM'S
ANNUAL CANDLE LIGHT SERVICE, DECEMBER 18, 2002.

This presentation is printed here, unedited and just as it was given. "T" represents Terry. "F" stands for Faris and these are my lines.

T: Welcome, everyone. We want to take this moment, first of all to thank the great people here at Oliver's for all they have done for us. Faris and I also want to thank them for giving us an opportunity to speak. We feel very honoured. I must also apologise for my voice. I have a bad head cold. Please bear with me.

We've been asked to share with you tonight our own story so you know some of our own grief, how we have learned to move forward in life, and how we approach the Christmas season. We hope to be able to offer you some ideas on how you can survive your losses, and know that there is hope and light and life for you.

F: PEACE. That is what Christmas is all about. "Peace on Earth", "Peace and goodwill", but also peace in your heart and soul. Christmas is a promise of peace. We can't promise that you'll find the peace you seek right here tonight, but maybe we can help you get closer to it. The source of our peace, strength, guidance, and healing is LOVE. I know that may sound corny to some of you, but it is the truth. And as we speak to you tonight you will see what we mean. Since I was a little girl, I understood that "GOD IS LOVE" I learned that it was easy to see God were ever I was because were ever there is an act of love, that is God. Real love. Unconditional, no strings attached. So when you ask, "Who is God?" well, God is Love. When you want to know, "Where is God?", God is every-where and in everyone. Where ever Love is. So whenever I speak of Love, I speak of God too. They are the same thing. That is my understanding and the source of my strength and positive outlook on things.

T: Our immediate family consists of 3 children. We always include the daughter we lost when we speak of our children. We'll speak of Jessie a bit later, but we want to mention Clint and Erin. Clinton our oldest and only son and Erin our youngest daughter are both young adults that we are very proud of. They are people with depth of character, integrity, faith, sincerity, and generosity. As a family, we have been travelling this path of grief and healing together, and even though we have dealt with this in many different ways, we all seem to be at about the same point. They have learned from us, but we have also learned a lot from each of them.

F: Terry and I started dating in High School. Only a few months later, Terry's Uncle died and I was touched to be asked to support Terry in his loss. A month later, some close friends and relatives of Terry's family were in a bad car crash some were killed and others badly injured. Again, I was there for my boyfriend who had lost some dear friends. But only a month later both my parents, Clint and Irene Swallow died in a car crash just outside Beaverlodge. Terry and his family were there for me. I was the oldest of 5 kids and over the years we each dealt with our loss in different ways, but what got us through was all the love we received from so many. I was especially lucky because I had found my life partner and his family welcomed me as their own. They taught me so much about life, but they also confirmed for me how amazing the love of family and friends could be – that amazing unconditional love from my own family and then from the family that has become my own, the Atkinsons. I was given the wonderful gift of Faith from my Parents. A strong faith and a love and appreciation of life. I know God to be the source of all love and that has helped to sustain me in times of great sorrow ever since. It helped me to survive the loss of my parents for I could see that love through so many caring people who guided me through life. And I wasn't easy to deal with. I was young and the pain and shock of loosing my life as I had known it was very hard. I was moody, angry and confused. I didn't understand that other people were grieving the loss of my parents and that their pain was deep too. As years went by, Terry and I shared many moments of joy and sorrow. The birth and growth of our children, making new friends, & celebrating achievements, but also the loss of many loved ones along the way.

T: It hasn't been long since the loss of Jessie, but even since her loss, we have lost others that bring grief fresh into our lives too. A friend's suicide, then Erin's best friend Jenny Carr to suicide as well. This one was particularly painful as we had grown to love Jenny so much. She was a lot like Jessie in many ways, even looked like her, and she was helping to fill the void left by Jessie. In 2001, I lost three first cousins all under the age of 40, and most recently, we lost a friend's 17-year-old son to suicide November 4th this year and Faris' maternal grandmother this November as well.

F: We've all heard it before, that there is life after death, our loved ones are in a better place, they'live on in heaven and similar statements. Hearing it said is one thing, believing it is blind faith and knowing it to be true is a blessing, but that doesn't make the pain of missing them any less. It's hard to see that "they are in a better place" when you feel that there would be no better place than right here in your arms. It's the missing them that hurts so much.

From left: Erin (Winkie), Jenny Carr, Jessie Jean. Erin would lose Jessie to suicide two months after this picture was taken, and Jenny 15 months later.

T: As I said before, we were blessed with three children. Clinton came first in 1980, then two years later Jessie Jean and then 19 months after that, Erin. Clint was a busy boy but a good boy. Erin was a sweet little girl and no trouble at all. Jessie was high maintenance. A gorgeous child who would light up a room from the moment she was born, and as she turned into a woman she caused heads to turn. But she was work right from the start. She was highly intelligent, a high achiever, sensitive, intuitive, and highly emotional. She was known for her temper tantrums as a girl and her intolerance to take any guff as a woman. She stood up for herself and others and spoke her mind. She was an excellent writer and extremely creative, well loved, but she had a dark side. A black cloud of despair in her heart she didn't know how to handle and we certainly were at a loss ourselves. We didn't recognise her problem as a medical one, DEPRESSION, until her Grade 9 year when she first attempted suicide. As a result, we learned about depression together as a family. It was an uphill battle to say the least. We learned first hand the seriousness and complexity of the disease. We tried to find help from any and all sources we had available to us. But we lost the battle. Two days before graduation, May 25, 2000, she shot herself in our home.

F: I remember the last time I saw her. I am so glad that the last words we spoke were I love you and good night. We have a game at our house. One of us says I love you and the other says, I love you more. That may be it, or in the case of Jessie and I that night it went a little further with nope, yep, and so on. What a blessing. To have hugged her for a nice long slow cuddle, rocking in each others arms, a kiss and those wonderful words being our last moments together. We did that often, but this time, that is a lasting and comforting memory.

T: I had spoken to Jessie the night before she died. Before going to bed, I checked in on her as she did home work. Sometimes we had trouble talking to each other. It was at times difficult for me to communicate with her, but sometimes we just clicked. Like the time just her and I went sledding in the mountains. She rode well on that big machine and took great pride in out-riding some of the men out there! It was great fun! She was so pleased with herself. There was the time I was sick and needed to go to Edmonton. She drove so I could rest. At 16 years old, she was confident and handled my extended cab 4x4 like a Pro!

We were so much alike, some times we butted heads... so it makes those good times so special. I enjoyed teaching her things she took interest in. She was so quick to learn. She loved to go Quadding with friends and family and was good at that too. Special times. Precious memories. Like the time she convinced me to go shopping with her for her Grad dress in April 2000. I was happy to be able to do something special with my daughter. I was out of my element, and uncomfortable while the sales woman and her were discussing how she needed to have the dress taken out to fit her chest. She was well endowed. Jessie, the sales lady and I all laughed having a father sharing a moment like that with his little girl. It's a memory I wouldn't trade for anything. Jessie had the most infectious laugh. When she laughed, you couldn't help it. She made you laugh too!

F: I'll never forget how time seemed to stand still when I heard she was gone. Everything was like it was in slow motion. I learned that it was our son Clint who had found her, called 911 and did CPR and another pain struck my heart. I needed to tell my sisters and brother. I needed all my family around me, and although some were close by in GP, Beaverlodge, Hythe and Goodfare, Some were far away in BC, and our baby Erin was in a private catholic school in Saskatchewan and still didn't know. We told her together over the phone while she had friends, teachers and clergy around her.

T: Jessie loved to shoot. I taught her. I taught her about gun safety, and she used to like to go partridge hunting. I remember going to the firing range with her Junior High phys. ed. class as a parent supervisor. She promptly out shot all the guys there that day. When I first learned she was gone, I felt like my heart had been torn right out.

F: Each of us think back on the moment we learned of the death of our loved ones and carry that thought with us, but more often we will remember special moments with them. We all have regrets. We wish that "If only . . ." and "Why didn't I . . ." But we all have great memories too. Instead of dwelling on the "woulda, shoulda, couldas" that can poison our souls, we should try and focus on the happy memories that give us strength.

T: We thank God everyday for the boundless outpouring of love given to us after loosing Jessie. Very wonderful memories. Very uplifting memories. Some of you have shared such memories with me. Like when friends lost a son days before Christmas several years ago. They had been busy up 'til then and hadn't got a tree up. Now they were grieving and their hearts weren't in it. When all at once her two brothers burst through the door with a tree in tow saying, "the big guy (referring to their nephew) would want you to have a tree." This is one of a mother's lasting and comforting memories . . . built by an act of love.

Our family had people open their homes, hearts, and souls sharing their many gifts with us. Our home was looked after, *and our hearts and souls were looked after too*, by all the very many friends and family that surrounded us. Acts of love all around us.

F: I have never felt so blessed as when I realized the depth and extent of how much we are loved. I took the almost 400 cards we had received and strung them on string like streamers all over the house. I had a "shrine" on our dining room table and in Jessie's room. Our house was open to all her friends, even if we weren't home. Looking back at it, we made new friends and built a larger family in the growth of the relationships with our children's friends and some of their parents. The kids help us to feel young and we have grown to love each of them dearly. Some feel like they are our own kids! And we know they love us too.

I have always been open with feelings and always analyze myself and ask myself why I feel as I do. This experience was no different. I looked inward to try to discover who I am again because I felt so changed. I have had moments when I have felt like I was lost and floundering, but I value this gift of life so deeply and the outpouring of love so profoundly, that a sense of peace, joy and hope are never far away from my heart.

T: I had a harder time climbing out of the darkness. At times I wanted to give up. I was tired of feeling so bad. My health went down hill. I was so ill I felt as though I was going to die. My body and my soul were as low as they had ever been. I didn't think I was going to survive and I wasn't sure I even wanted to any more. If it hadn't been for the love and emotional support of my family and friends, I may not have made it through.

Faris was grieving her own way, and it was so different from mine. I couldn't understand it at first. It would have been easy to resent her for being so positive sometimes, and not grieving like me. But we learned that we needed to grieve in different ways and to recognise and support each other in that. It could have torn us apart as we travelled down paths that seemed to be heading in opposite directions sometimes. But the recognition of that pulled us together instead of apart.

Another thing happened that we learned from. We would walk on eggshells around each other. It seemed that when I was having a particularly bad day, Faris would be having a particularly good one. I wouldn't say how bad *I* was feeling because I thought that it would bring *her* down. I didn't want to *ruin* her good day. The same thing would happen with her. Then we realized . . . everything seems to happen for a reason . . . why do you suppose we didn't seem to have a bad day at the same time? Because, you see, I would be strong enough and happy enough to help Faris through her bad day, and she could do the same for me when I was down and she was up. Erin would go to her room, hide away to cry over the loss of her sister and the loss of her best friend. We realized . . . it gives us a sense of purpose as parents, we draw strength from being able to hold her, comfort her and share her grief with her. *She* learned that it helped us to help her, so she doesn't hide her feelings away *as much* anymore. The lesson is to share with each other. It is very healing and pulls you together instead of apart.

F: We are always missing Jessie. We are always thinking of her and it honours us to know that you are thinking of her too, and missing her. We want to hear that from others. If you feel that way too, don't be afraid to tell your friends and family it would help you to talk about the one you miss. I have learned that sharing the memories I have of my parents with people who loved them made them feel close to me again, for some one else's memories were like learning something new about my parents. It helped to keep them alive in my heart. That was so much more evident with Jessie. I had no idea the extent of the impact she had on so many people. It was like learning something new and wonderful about Jessie for days and weeks and months after she was gone and it helped me to feel that she was still with us because of all the new and wonderful experiences we were learning about her. We developed a strong bond with people that she had touched in some way…people we never knew before. We saw many amazing things happen, true colours of people, extraordinary results occurred as a direct effect of Jessie's passing. Beauty came out of the ugliness of her death, like ripples in a pond, and we are still feeling the results of that.

Our priorities have changed. Our fast-paced lifestyle has slowed down so that we can enjoy smelling the roses along the way. I have discovered who I am. I feel connected to everyone and everything in the Universe. That is humbling and empowering all at once. I am not brave or courageous, I just see how wonderful life is, I am so blessed because I know how blessed I am. But each of us is different. Your needs are different than mine. Our losses are varied, you may not have the love around you as we did. You may be at odds with family or friends.

Life can be looking like a deep dark hole you can't seem to see the way out of. Remember this. There needs to be balance in the universe. For every negative there is an equal positive. For the amount of pain you feel now, there is an equal joy waiting for you to experience. There is a ladder in that hole of despair with you. You just need to find it, recognise it and use it to pull yourself up out of the hole with.

T: This was an especially important lesson for me and hard to learn. When I lost my Dad, I felt like this. I'm strong. I'm a man and I don't need anyone's help. I have been through tough times before. Only the weak go for help. Besides, my brother and I have to be strong for Mom and my sisters. The pain, anger and grief was still there, but I was going to fight my way through it and I was determined to beat it. We were going to have an Auction Sale. I knew Dad would have wanted me to do it. He was so proud of me from the first time I called an Auction Sale. I needed to be in control of my emotions and even though it was one of the most painful and difficult things I had to do to that point, I did it.

But the loss of Jessie was too much to bear. I crumbled under the weight of it all and I realized that everyone needs help sometime. *It isn't weakness, it is wisdom.* Because I *accepted* help, I have learned how to *give it* much better than I did before. *I am more aware.* I am able to be *strong* for some one else because I learned how to *accept strength from others.*

Accepting help didn't make me less a man...it made me a better one.

F: Another lesson I learned was not to try to carry everyone else's pain. I had my own, but I was trying to carry everyone else's for them. I had to realize that they are still hurting just as much and I am stumbling under the weight of the added burden I was trying to carry. So I had to let it go. I learned to support, love, but not to hurt for them too. I have enough hurt of my own. It is hard to do, but if you can do it, it helps you take giant leaps on your healing path.

We still have a small "shrine" in our living room for Jessie. Every year on her perennial day, May 25th, we have a bonfire party at our house when all her friends and some of our friends and family, friend's parents, Clint and Erin's friends all gather and party 'til dawn. We usually have kids sleeping in every room on couches and in corners. We feed them breakfast, and sometimes even lunch before they all go home. We have so much fun and share how we still miss Jessie, reminisce about times with her, and so on. It is a great time.

Every day I find that I am wearing something of Jessie's. I don't plan it that way, I just seem to do it. Today, these are her boots. I guess it helps me to keep her close. I wore a yellow ribbon for suicide prevention for along time, then it was a butterfly angel pin, now I don't seem to need any of those things, but I still find that I wear something of hers every day. When we write a card or letter and sign all our names to it, I draw a little butterfly for Jessie. I discovered that when I write a J for Jessie and mirror a J for Jean beside it, it makes a little butterfly, one of her favourite things.

T: Jessie had made a necklace out of one of my small very expensive wrenches. It was very creative and unique. She wore it a lot when she was in Junior High. I found it in her room not long ago, and I now have it hanging from the rear view mirror in my truck. Grieving and healing are *not* two separate things . . . they are intertwined . . . & just as we will always grieve for Jessie, we will also continue to find new ways of healing. Every day is another step in our journey of the healing process. What I expect is to find a way to be happy for the moment and find strength to move on to the next moment, and the next.

F: Christmas has been hard to deal with since I lost my parents. Anxiety has always been part of Christmas since my Parents died. Preparations, so many events, gatherings and parties to attend or plan, the financial burdens, little time to just reflect, relax and enjoy the beauty of the season. Together as a couple, and then a family, we had to develop new traditions and I tried to incorporate some of the traditions my parents had instilled in me. I write Christmas newsletters in rhyme as my parents did, I try and go to church services during advent and especially on Christmas Eve, it helps me take that needed time for reflection and pause for a time to remember what Christmas is…not what I perceive it to be. And it makes going to church so much better when my family joins me. That is *Christmas past*. Christmas with Jessie, when my family was complete included those traditions carried over from my parents, like not putting presents under the tree until everyone was in bed Christmas eve, plus some of our own traditions, and some Atkinson family traditions mixed in. But a carry over of grief in missing being able to share the season with my parents still made Christmas an anxious and stressful time of year. But having the kids to share it with made it a happy and wonderful time.

T: Christmas is sometimes hard enough *without* loss. I dreaded the stress that the season brought on me to make sure we had enough under the tree. But then I would remember that it is a season of coming together as family, enjoying each other, having fun doing things as a family. By Christmas Eve, I was excited and looked forward to the morning and spending the day with the family. But now it is *"Christmas present,"* Christmases without Jessie. For Christmas 2000, our first Christmas without her, Faris started a new tradition.

F: I found a ceramic doll with long dark curls and big blue eyes wearing a golden winter suit. I took off her hat and made her a halo of gold and fashioned her some gossamer butterfly wings. It is our Jessie angel that takes her place atop our Christmas tree now. And her Christmas stocking is laid out with everyone else's too. Sometimes a little note from one of us might find it's way into the sock, or a flower or some other such acknowledgement that she is still a big part of being with us this day. This year I took a few sprigs of holly and placed them on her grave. I do this mostly for her friends to let them know that they aren't alone in thinking of her and that she is included in some small way in this season of joy.

T: This year, our daughter Erin suggested that she really could care less if anything was under the tree and would be much happier if we just did something fun together as a family. We used to go to the mountains as the entire Atkinson clan and make a day of tree hunting. We have a lot of great memories of those days. This was a tradition. Our lives got busier, the kids grew up, and then we all bought artificial trees. No more tree hunts. We haven't really replaced those good outings yet. This year Faris & I are thinking of going out on Bradshaw's lake by Beaverlodge for a family day of skating and bonfires like we used to do in the winter when the kids were all small. Maybe it'll be a *new* Christmas time tradition! The Love and support of family and friends is what the season should bring us. Not more heartache. I think it is so important to include the ones you lost in Christmas with you. You're thinking of them anyway. Be open about it.

F: Remember, each of us hurts. Share that with the ones you love who are hurting too. Remember we all carry feelings of guilt, fear, shame, regret, and horrible loss. We all need to be helped through it at times and we all need to be able to help at times. These two needs are very important, so do not neglect either one. Take the help when you need it, and give the help when you are able. If you get nothing else from this sharing tonight, I hope you will walk away knowing that you are not alone. There are people who care and who can help you heal. If they are not already around you, go looking for them. There are support groups, church groups, councillors, clergy, friends and family, so many people who truly care. Don't be afraid to ask for help, or to accept it when it is offered.

You are someone's child, no matter how old you are. My husband and I are 46 but we are expected to call Terry's Mom when we get home from her place to let her know we are safe. My great grandmother lost a young son and wept for him 'til the day she died at 92 years old. Once you are a child, you will always be a part of your parent's very being. To have to bury a child is the worst thing a parent ever has to do, no matter if that child is an infant, a parent, a grandparent, or a beautiful young adult in the prime of their life. Of all our losses, this is the worst. This is the one that shattered us. And we continue to suffer losses. Like we said before, Erin's best friend Jenny was a joy in our lives. She was so special and so sweet almost a replacement for the daughter we lost. Losing her to suicide twisted the knife in our already wounded hearts. So many more dear people we have lost in the past two years. Most recently we grieve the loss of my friend's 17-year-old son, and my sweet grandmother. But our sorrow is not any deeper than yours, pain is pain, hurt is hurt and it is real and powerful and devastating no matter who it is we have lost or how. How we grieve and how we chose to deal with that grief is very personal and very individual. I chose not to wallow in it. I did for a while, but decided to stop feeling like that and count my blessings, appreciate life and the lessons I have been given and to move on. I try to find something positive in every situation. That is me, and it has worked for me. It may not work for you. But what will?

T: One thing I can tell you is that you won't know what will work for you unless you allow yourself time to think about it. You should try to take time to be alone in a quiet place where you feel that you can listen to your heart. Maybe it's on a tractor making rounds in a field, maybe it's on a snow machine on a mountain top, maybe by a lake, or in a garden, in a good book, in a church pew, wherever it is, go there, listen to your heart. This is especially important at this time of year. We are stressed and we are grieving. No wonder we feel as bad as we do sometimes. It is so important that you try and find a place to stop. Sit. Rest. Reflect on life, love, loss, joy, sorrow, and the wonder of it all. Pray, meditate, or just listen to nature around you, what ever it takes to find some peace. Another thing you can try and do is to recognise the miracles around you. They may be small and well disguised, but if you are paying attention, they are everywhere. A phone call from someone at just the right time, a well placed rainbow, a songbird, the thoughts of a friend, a certain song on the radio, a butterfly, what ever it may be, you'll recognise it because of it's timing and the way you feel once you realize it for what it is . . . a gift from heaven.

F: So go in *peace* and know that you are never alone in this. You can't run away from grief, it follows you. Meet it head on and mould it into your pathway to healing. Christmas will be different this year and for years to come. Don't ignore that. Don't ignore them, the one's you will miss. They live in your hearts and in your memories. Include them into Christmas. It will be hard, the days leading up to Christmas and Christmas day itself.

You might cry. That's ok. Share it. And try to find joy in the blessings that will be all around you . . . *they are each other and the love you share.*

We'll leave you with a famous quote from the story "A Christmas Carol."

T & F: *"God Bless us, everyone"*

Terry and Faris at the Columbia Ice Fields, July 2004.

Three Little Poems

FLOWER OF LIFE

Feel the goodness in all forms of life
Love all things; let go of strife
Open your petals; let love flow in
Widen the gap; let love grow within
Erase the scars of the past
Rest in the assurance that only love lasts

Own your self worth in spite of what others say
Find again the peace in your day

Live your potential; let the world know
Into your self, let a new energy flow
Find out you have so much to give
Embrace love; laugh and live

Be joyous and free: Be all that you are and ever could be

—Eileen Finch Cain 10/27/02
(Printed with permission)

YOU'RE THERE TOO
For Jessie

When I dance in the rain, I'm dancing with you,

When I sing really loud, you're there too,

When I cry at night, you're there with me,

When I'm all alone, you're all I see.

You're in the wind that touches my hair,

You're the stars that shine without a care,

I can see your face when the moon shines

And on the water's glint a million times.

You're carried on butterfly's wings and in the setting sun,

You're the fresh smell when a rainstorm is done.

I'm glad to have you surrounding my world,

In everything I do and everywhere I look.

It helps me cope

With the precious life God took.

—*Erin Atkinson*

JUST FOR TODAY

Just for today, for I cannot promise
That I can do it tomorrow.
Just for today then, the whole day through
I will rise above my sorrow.

Today and just today alone
I'll find joy everywhere I look
I'll see beauty in unlikely spots
And read or write in at least one book.

I may not be around tomorrow
I may not have the strength or grace
So today and just for today
I'll make the best of this time and space.

I'll be generous and compassionate
I'll thank the source of love as I awake
I'll not be idle, but resourceful
I'll watch every step I take.

Just for today, and only then
As I sit and as I plan
I will try to be an instrument
And do good wherever I can.

Today I start with this simple rhyme
To remind me to stay in the light
To temper my words with wisdom
And to love with all my might.

Just for today, for I cannot promise
That I can do it tomorrow
Just for today then, all day through
I will rise above my sorrow.

—Faris Jean

APPENDIX C

Signs and Symptoms of Depression

The following signs and symptoms alone may not tell you that you have depression. However, if you display more than one of these and something has occurred in your life that tends to lead to depression, it would be wise to see your physician, a mental-health professional, or other qualified and reputable health-care specialist.

Changes in eating and sleeping patterns: In some cases, a person will gravitate to "comfort foods" with high-fat, high-carbohydrate and high-sugar content. Using food as an escape, such a person tends to gain weight. Others may find they have lost their appetite and begin to lose weight.

Some may find it difficult to fall asleep. Insomnia is common in people suffering from depression. Sometimes, however, falling asleep may not be the initial problem; rather, the depressed person wakes in the night and is unable to fall back to sleep. Others want to sleep all the time. It seems they do nothing but sleep, complain of feeling tired, or talk about how they want or need to sleep. Remember, these are *changes* in sleep patterns. If you normally have restless sleep, it may be related to something else, or it may be your normal sleep pattern. Any change in that pattern, however, may indicate that something is going on in your life that warrants a closer look.

Change in attitude or outlook on life: Imagine a person (maybe it is you) who has always had a positive outlook on life. This is the optimist, the Pollyanna personality, usually cheerful and easygoing. Such people may be patient and understanding most of the time, but now you notice they have become irritable and drawn inward. They can't seem to find joy in anything any more. They seem like a different person. This is an example of a change in attitude. A person can have a bad day or even a bad week, but if this personality change lingers to the point where you wonder where the person you used to know has gone, that should send up a little red flag.

Feeling tired and lacking energy: A decline in energy can be related to the change in sleep patterns, but it sometimes can occur in people who have no obvious problems sleeping. They just can't find the energy to do the things they could do before. They are dragging. They would rather lie on the couch than go for their usual walk to the mailbox. Whatever it is, they no longer seem to have the spring in their step that they once had, and furthermore, they don't really care.

Increased use of alcohol or drugs: For some, television or video games are a good escape. Others find comfort in food. There are many ways to run away from reality for a while. But some find that intoxicants are a great way to escape their feelings. It gives them a temporary feeling of euphoria, sweeps them away from their reality for a while, and helps them flee the wretchedness they feel in their lives. They can also use it as an excuse for their behaviour and hide from responsibility for their actions. Unfortunately, not only does this not give them the relief they desire; it can make the problem worse. Alcohol and some drugs are depressants. But whatever the intoxicant, it may give only a temporary fix. Later, coming down off the high, the feelings of sadness, despair and hopelessness can actually increase. The original problem is compounded by drug- or alcohol-induced health, social, and financial problems, and so on. The sufferer doesn't think of consequences, however. He or she is just trying to find a way to numb the pain, even for a little while.

Loss of interest in work, school, or hobbies: Things people have done well at or enjoyed, taken pride in doing, and found stimulating, no longer hold those rewards. Instead of looking forward to an event or activity, they dread it; they'll make excuses not to participate. They just don't want to do it any more. Again, there is a possible link between poor sleep, lack of energy, poor nutrition, and sour attitude. The relationship between the causes and symptoms may seem clearer when you understand some of the causes of depression.

Withdrawing from family, friends, and social activities: No interest, no energy, and now isolation. It takes energy to be sociable. Sometimes depressed people don't even want to talk to anyone. They don't answer the phone and pretend they aren't home. They'll pretend they're asleep or sick—anything to keep from having to visit with anyone. Some people prefer the pleasure of their own company to that of anyone else. That is normal for them, but if isolation is a change in their normal behaviour, then something is likely wrong.

Lack of concentration: Normally, the depressive could get through a class at school, a task at work, or a project with no problem, but now it is increasingly difficult to stay focused on the task. This can be a source of great frustration, and the anxiety involved can make it worse. They know something is wrong, but they can't pin it down and don't make the association between their lack of concentration and their feeling blue. This is a subtle sign and can sometimes be missed, as it is often rationalized away as being tired, hung over, distracted, or something else.

Taking unnecessary risks: This is a change. All at once you notice that someone seems to have no regard for the consequences of their actions. They do things that could harm them and they seem to relish "flirting with death". Some people are natural thrill-seekers; they love the rush of adrenaline and they seem to take risks with their life. But these people do it to enhance their living; they have no intention of dying. They take all safety precautions, train, study, prepare for the risks, whether it is ice climbing or skydiving, caving, or whatever. That is who they are, and that is different from the depressed person taking unnecessary risks. Unnecessary risk taking comes when someone participates in an activity that they almost hope will hurt them. They do it to enhance the chance of death, not to enhance the thrill of living. There are no precautions, just spontaneous impulsive actions. Speeding down winding roads with no seatbelt and under the influence of alcohol is an unnecessary risk. But not all people who do that are looking to die; they may just think they are invincible. Again, this behaviour may not indicate depression on its own; it must be placed in context.

APPENDIX D

Some Major Causes
of Depression

Negative Changes: This usually refers to loss. It may be loss of a loved one through death, divorce, or separation. It could be loss of a life style, a job, a home, or one's health. It could be loss of a part of the body through trauma or surgery, loss of memory, or loss of a sense such as hearing or sight. Whatever the loss, it may trigger despair. If a person has a hard time coping with a loss, it can lead to depression. Health problems are a common cause of depression. People who suffer heart disease, stroke, Parkinson's disease, or hypothyroidism to name a few, are often afflicted with depression.

Poor Nutrition: Healthy eating starts with moderation and progresses to limiting the amount of processed foods that you eat. The more something is handled, prepared, packaged, and processed, the worse it is for you. But certain foods seem to compound sadness and can lead to depression. A diet high in sugar and caffeine can be especially detrimental to someone already suffering with "the blues". A diet high in Omega-3, -6 and –9 fatty acids, selenium, folic acid, vitamin B complex, and trace minerals can help the body cope (see Appendix H for a book on this subject). Healthy eating helps promote organ function, and that can be important in the functioning of the brain and other nervous tissue, thyroid glands, adrenal glands, pancreas and liver. Good circulation is also a benefit, as is a healthy digestive system and effective metabolism. Our bodies are extremely complex, and everything is connected. Healthy eating provides energy and helps maintain a healthy weight, healthy hair and healthy skin. This is all–important for our self-image, and that plays a part in how we feel about ourselves. Along with diet, exercise is important as it helps promote production of endorphins, which can stimulate "happy" or positive feelings. Consuming alcohol while depressed is like throwing gasoline on a fire to put it out. It makes things worse. Tobacco is also a bad idea as the chemicals ingested or inhaled wreak havoc on an already-stressed system. Remember, everything is connected. Smoking gives the sensation of relaxation, but like alcohol, it fools you and can actually compound the problem. Chewing tobacco is just as detrimental as smoking it. If you think not, think again!

Social Factors: How a person fits into society is a huge issue. Peer pressure can play a role. Constant bullying can lead to serious depression. Financial difficulties, employment problems, cultural issues, lack or perceived lack of support can all play a big role in despair. Relationships with friends, family, partners, and lovers can be rocky, non-existent, or even dangerous: Social factors can drive a person into deep depression. Major life changes can stretch our coping skills to the point where they snap.

Biochemical Changes: This can refer to hormonal or neurotransmitter changes. In some cases, no change occurs; the person may have been born with a tendency to neurotransmitter dysfunction. But changes in hormonal balance can often make a person especially prone to depression. Puberty, menopause, and post-partum are the obvious times one can think of. Post–partum depression occurs after a woman gives birth, when she is going through major hormonal changes. For some women, the normal swings of emotion and periods of anxiety and sadness become accentuated and lead to full-blown clinical depression.

Neurotransmitters are vital to the transmission of electric signals along our nerves, sending crucial messages through our bodies and brains. Nerve cells do not touch each other. There is a small gap between them called the synapse or synaptic gap. Neurotransmitters are chemicals that enable the electrical impulses to cross the gap and reach the next nerve cell along down line, one after the other, until the message reaches its destination. In many depressed people, production of these transmitters is diminished or the transmitters themselves become less effective. The lack of properly functioning neurotransmitters is the thread that links many of our symptoms together: lethargy, sleep problems, loss of appetite, and concentration.

Research shows that, in many cases, the longer someone suffers from undiagnosed and untreated depression, the more likely that person is to develop biochemical problems (if that wasn't the original cause).

SAD: Seasonal Affective Disorder (SAD) is a biochemical change that occurs during the winter months. It causes an extreme case of the blues and signs of depression. It is most common in January and February, but can establish itself as early as August or September and linger until April or May. Symptoms will have occurred in the past two years with no "non-seasonal" episodes. In other words, the person feels "normal," with no real depression issues during the summer months.

Melatonin is a natural hormone produced by the pineal gland. When the sun goes down and darkness comes, the pineal gland goes to work. As melatonin production rises, you begin to feel less alert and your body temperature starts to fall. Usually, melatonin levels drop as the day dawns, and sometimes it is so low in the daytime that it's barely detectable to Doctors. Melatonin levels go hand in hand with the light and dark cycles for people. This ebb and flow of melatonin levels becomes abnormal in people suffering from SAD, with higher levels persisting through the short daylight hours of winter.

Often people with SAD will crave sugary or starchy foods and will show other symptoms of depression during the winter, but the symptoms will subside through late spring and summer.

Young people and women seem to be at a higher risk of this form of depression than others, but anyone can be affected. Light is often recommended as a therapy for SAD. Sunlight is the best, but other special lights can be used.

What to Do
If You Are Depressed

I f you feel depressed, see your physician or a mental-health professional. They will help determine the intensity of your depression
and will support your efforts to regain your mental health. Most
health-care workers have grown to understand the need for a holistic
approach to mental health. They know that everyone is different in
what they respond to and how. There is a need not only to focus on
mental well being, but also on emotional, spiritual, and physical health
as a part of treatment. It is important to work together with the professionals to find what will work for you. Some find great success in
proper diet, an exercise regime, spiritual support, relaxation techniques, and eliminating stressors as far as possible.

But if biochemical changes have occurred, more aggressive treatment is required. Conventional medication is one option, and in extreme cases, this may be the best choice. Recent research, however,
has shown that in some people, especially youth, conventional
anti-depressants can actually exacerbate the problem. But alternative
or natural "medication" can be effective for many people. These include St. John's Wort, SamE and L-tyrosine. These compounds
should be taken only under the supervision of a reputable naturopathic
health-care provider. It is important that you understand that just one
treatment method probably won't work. You need to change all as-
pects of your health-care regimen and make some lifestyle changes for
best results. There are different types of depression—unipolar and bi-
polar, for example—and there are other depression-related illnesses
such as anxiety disorder. Each disorder and each individual will respond to different treatments: counselling, meditation, prayer, music,
pet therapy, light therapy, massage. Do whatever it takes to attain your
mental health and keep trying until you find what works for you.
There are many resources available to assist you (see Appendix H), so
don't give up.

How to Help a Friend

There are three things you can do to help a friend: Talking to him or her, listening, and getting help.

Talking:
- Plan to talk with your friend at a time and place where you won't be interrupted.
- Ask him (or her, as the case may be) how he is doing and how he is feeling.
- Tell him what changes you have noticed in him, or what it is that concerns you. Let him know you are worried about him.
- Encourage him to talk about what is going on in his life.
- Ask if he has been depressed, and find out how long he has been feeling that way.
- Ask about how bad things are for him, and ask how this is affecting his life. If he describes feelings of depression, hopelessness, or wishing he were dead, that leads you to the next question.
- Are things so bad that he has thought about ending his life? Ask if he has been feeling suicidal. (You won't be putting the idea in his head or making the situation worse by asking. However, you will show that you are willing to listen and willing to help. Your questions show that you care.)
- If your friend says "yes", you need to tell someone who can help. Get his agreement to talk to someone right now. He (or she) should not be left alone. (See Getting Help below.)

Listening:
- Show you care about him by "active listening".
- Listen openly, without judging what he is saying. Often just being able to talk about problems helps change a person's mood.
- If he doesn't want to talk to you, let him know that you will check with him later and he can talk to you any time.

- Listen to his problems and see whether you can determine where the greatest pressure is coming from.
- Find out what he has tried to do to cope with his situation or methods he has used to cope with similar situations in the past. Is there someone or something he can turn to for support?
- Listen without immediately offering advice. Don't think you need to have an answer for your friend's problems.
- Don't make promises about how everything will be okay. Take your friend seriously.

Getting Help:
- Let him know there is help for his depression. Even though his situation may seem hopeless and overwhelming, things can change and he can get through it.
- Encourage him to talk to someone rather than to struggle with his problems alone. Talk about available resources and supports (Appendix H).
- If he is willing to talk to a counsellor or someone else, offer to go with him for support. If he goes alone, check later to see how it went.
- Talk about what he is going to do to make things better (spend less time alone, make an appointment with a doctor, get exercise, or talk to a counsellor). Have him repeat the plan back to you.
- If he won't go for help and is really depressed, and if you are unsure what to do, contact someone you can trust for help and advice. A crisis line can give you assistance or information on resources. You might also try your local mental-health clinic or suicide-prevention centre for more information or help.
- A suicidal person who has a plan and the means available to carry out that plan, should not be left alone.
- Encourage him to call you or someone else he trusts if what he is planning to do for help doesn't work out. Find out whom he would talk to if he is feeling out of control or in a crisis.

APPENDIX G
Some Facts on Depression

*And yet in certain of these cases there is mere anger and grief and sad
dejection of mind . . . . Those affected with melancholy are not every one of
them affected according to one particular form, but they are suspicious of
poisoning, or flee to the desert from misanthropy, or turn superstitious, or
contract a hatred of life. Or if at any time a relaxation takes place, in most
cases hilarity supervenes. The patients are dull or stern, dejected or
unreasonably torpid . . . they also become peevish, dispirited and start up
from a disturbed sleep.*

—ARATEUS (AD 150)

Depression has been with us for a very long time. Our under-standing of it has evolved, and our attitudes are changing with that understanding. However, there is still a lot we don't know and a lot more work to do in changing attitudes. We know that depression is not just mood, behaviour or attitude, but an actual mental illness, and more people need to understand this.

Over the summer of 2003, we have heard about SARS and West Nile Virus and Mad Cow Disease. The media have been full of it, in some cases using the word "epidemic." This has ruffled my feathers, I can tell you. The fact is, if they want to know what is ravaging our population with an epidemic, it is mental illness, not the least of which are depression and depression-related illnesses—but rarely do you ever hear of this in the news.

The World Health Organization (WHO) predicted in a 2003 state-ment that by 2020 depression and related mental illness would be the number one disabling condition in developed countries, surpassing heart disease and strokes.

More people die by suicide than from war and homicide combined. In the year 2000, more than 815,000 people died by their own hands worldwide—one suicide every forty seconds.

Canada has an especially high rate of suicide. Based on 1999 statis-tics, approximately 4,000 Canadians each year die by suicide. It is the leading cause of death for women aged 30–34 years and for men aged 25–29 and 40–44. It is the second leading cause of death among youth aged 15–24. This is a serious social and public health problem that costs Canadians more than $3 billion annually. Self-inflicted injury or death cost Americans an estimated $44 billion in 2002. Alberta is one of the regions in Canada where suicide is highest. In some years, our area, Alberta's Northwest, leads the rest of our province in suicide rates. The leading cause of death for all ages in Alberta is injury, and when looking at the types of injury deaths from 1986–1999, suicide was the leading cause, followed by motor-vehicle collisions. These two made up more than half of the Injury deaths in Alberta.

Of all the people who die by suicide, between 80% and 95% were known to have suffered with depression.

In the United States, the government has commissioned a National Suicide Prevention Strategy. We have no such thing in Canada, although several of us are lobbying for it. The Canadian Association for Suicide Prevention is working with other groups to develop a blueprint for a national strategy.

In October 2003:
- Alberta and Quebec had provincial strategies;
- New Brunswick had a suicide-prevention coordinator;
- The Northwest Territories and Nunavut had activities aimed at suicide prevention;
- There have been two major reports that discuss suicide among First Nations and Inuit Communities (statistics show that the aboriginal people of Canada have the highest rates of suicide in the country);
- The rest of the provinces have community groups and associations engaged in suicide prevention, intervention and "postvention" (bereavement) activities.

Look for a Suicide Prevention Program in your area.

For more information, the Internet can be an amazing resource. Start with some of the websites and resources I have listed for you in Appendix H. Some are for information only, but most are places where you can get both information and help.

APPENDIX H

Resources

Many websites on depression and suicide are available, but it can be overwhelming to find what you need by an Internet search. With the help of the wonderful staff at the Suicide Prevention Resource Centre in Grande Prairie, Alberta, I am providing you with a place to start.

Help/Crisis – Are You in Crisis Now?
- International help lines www.suicide-helplines.org under "find a crisis line near you" scroll to your country and so on. Or you can click on "helping a friend" for guidance.
- National Kids Help: 1-800-668-6868
  www.kidshelp.sympatico.ca
- National Parents Help: 1-888-603-9100
  www.metanoia.org/imhs/crisis.htm
- Especially For Teens: www.yellowribbon.org
  or www.yellowribbon.ca
- Alberta Mental Health 1-877-303-2642
- In the USA call 1-800-suicide (784-2433)

Information on Depression, Suicide or Other Mental Illness
Besides being wonderful information resources, most of these sites also offer links to crisis assistance.
- www.med.ualberta.ca/acicr is the site of the Alberta Centre for Injury Control and Research. It is a very good site that includes a multitude of great links including Health Canada, National Safety Council (USA), World Health Organization, Statistics Canada and much more.
- www.nimh.nih.gov is a United States government site and has lots of information. It's an excellent resource for symptoms, diagnosis, and treatment of a variety of mental illnesses. It also has stories of depression and the article "Real Men, Real Depression."

- www.suicideprevention.ca The Canadian Association for Suicide Prevention has lots of wonderful info and interesting links, including one for crisis lines across the country.
- www.samaritans.org/talk/email.shtm This is a great place to go for e-mail support.
- www.afsp.org The American Foundation for Suicide Prevention is full of information and, like many of the other sites listed here, has survivor support.
- www.suicideinfo.ca is the Centre for Suicide prevention in Calgary Alberta, serving people in Alberta, across Canada and around the world..
- www.suicidology.org is an American association and has a wealth of information on support groups, crisis centres, prevention, and treatment for both the U.S. and Canada.
- www.healthpolitics.com is another great American site full of all kinds of health information. On 3/17/2004 they aired a radio program on Depression and Suicide that can be accessed on this site. It's worth a listen.

Seasonal Affective Disorder

Again, lots of great sites, and here are a few.
- www.sada.org.uk
- http://web.nami.org/helpline/sad.htm
- http://world.std.com/~halberst/contrib/sad.html
- http://healthyhighway.com

Stress Management

I typed "**stress management**" into a Search Engine and found a flood of sites on the subject. Any number of them is sure to have helpful ideas and information.

Suicide Bereavement

Most of the sites already mentioned have support for survivors.
- At www.afsp.org/index-1.htm you click on "Survivor."
- You might also try www.1000deaths.com/lists.html for online mutual-support groups.

- Suicide Awareness Voices of Education (SAVE) also has a site that may be helpful at www.save.org.

Naturopathic or Alternative Medicine Information
- One of the best sites I found was the site for the British Columbia Naturopathic Association www.bcna.ca.
- www.naturopathicassoc.ca belongs to the Canadian Naturopathic Association.
- A great site for naturopathic resources is www.aanmc.org/resources/index.php,
- www.todoinstitute.org covers Japanese psychology techniques.
- www.supplementsolutions.com/same.htm provides some information on one of the products that Jessie used and found very helpful. This site is selling the product as well. I would suggest that you do further research on your own via the Internet or conventionally, before you make any decision to try it.
- For information on L-Tyrosine www.healthy.net.
- 5-HTP, another alternative treatment for depression http://healthinfo.healthgate.com.

Consult a health care professional before trying any supplemental regime.

Reading
Bateson-Koch, Carolee, *Allergies, Disease in Disguise: How to heal your allergic condition permanently and naturally.* Alive Books, 1994.

Bloomfield, Harold M.D. *How to Heal Depression.* Prelude Press, 1994. Dr. Bloomfield explains that nutritional deficiencies are common in depressed people. His advice on healthy eating and nutritional supplements has helped some depressives. Maybe it will help you, too.

Ellis, Ron and Shea, Steven, *Over the Boards–The Ron Ellis Story.* Fenn Publishing, 2002. Ron tells of his professional hockey career and his struggle with depression after retiring from hockey.

Kubler-Ross, Elisabeth, *On death and Dying*. Macmillan, 1969, 1991. Also available on cassette.

Kushner, Harold S., *When Bad things Happen to Good People*. Schocken Books, 1981; Avon, 1989. Also available on cassette and in large-print edition.

Walsch, Neale Donald, *Conversations with God: an uncommon dialogue*. G.P. Putam's Sons 1996. Also available on cassette and in large-print edition.

(Jessie's treatment for candida, which literally cured her migraine headaches, was prescribed by Dr. Bateson-Koch, the chiropractor and medical doctor who wrote *Allergies, Disease in Disguise*. This book says that allergies can trigger many diseases and disorders, including depression. Lendon H. Smith, MD, writes in the foreword: "I believe that everyone suffers from some food sensitivity. The clues are in this book. Before the reader runs off to the psychiatrist because the doctor can find nothing wrong, the methods in this book should give some relief.")

For more reading on the subject matter of this book, search your library catalogue or ask a librarian for help

Healing and Grief Counselling
- Try healing through music or rhythms. Rob Smith, a grief counsellor in Grande Prairie, has a website on the subject at www.healingrhythms.ca.
- You don't have to be musical to find your heart's voice. Look at www.theheartsvoice.com.

Butterfly Symbolism:
- www.insects.org/ced4/butterfly_symbols.html or www.hkandro.net/anima._butterfly.htm to name only two of many. These are both great sites to learn about lepidopteral symbolism.

About the Author

Faris Jean Atkinson (nee Swallow) was born in Viking Alberta on April 4, 1956. Her parents Reverend Clinton George Swallow and Irene Jean Swallow (nee Lee) had five children. Faris is the oldest. In 1974, both parents were killed in a car crash.

In this book, Faris shares her story of loss and how she found joy in living through her relationships with her Creator, family, friends, nature and community.

In 1977, she married her high school sweetheart, Terry Atkinson. Together they had Clinton (1980), Jessie (1982) and Erin (1983). Faris holds an interest in music and enjoys singing. She also enjoys painting landscapes. Faris has, in the past, acted as a lay minister for the United Churches in Hythe, Wembley, Beaverlodge and Clairmont.

After the death of her daughter by suicide, Faris has picked up the banner for educating the public on depression and suicide. Through presentations, she speaks to students, youth groups, and adults on those topics.

Faris took training as an Emergency Medical Technician and worked in that field for close to five years with the Beaverlodge/Hythe Ambulance Service. Returning to school, she graduated from the Diploma Nursing Program at the Grande Prairie Regional College in 1993 and worked as a registered nurse in the community, industry and in acute care for two years. Since 1986 she has been instructing St. John Ambulance First Aid and became the Peace Region Area Manager for that organization in 1995. Leaving that position in February 2001, she continues to instruct on occasion, but also volunteers as a Branch Advisory Board member, and Brigade Member.

Faris has dedicated her life to caring for and helping people in need from all walks of life. She started writing as therapy for herself; to help her work through her grief, but if one person is influenced, feels comforted, finds joy, or relief or feels compelled to find love or inspired to help others, if one life is saved as a result of writing this book, then it has been *more* than worthwhile.